MW00581187

Daily Warm Up F
for
Bass Guitar

Methods
for
developing a daily practice routine
with
scales, modes & arpeggios.

Bass Tab Edition

by Steven Mooney

1st Edition October 2013

Print Edition   ISBN 978-1-937187-02-6
eBook Edition ISBN 978-1-937187-03-3

Library of Congress Control Number:

Musical Score : Fretted instruments & guitar
Musical Score : Studies & exercises, etudes

Layout and music engraving by Steven Mooney
Cover Design by Steven Mooney

Table of Contents.

Part 1.
FINGER CO ORDINATION AND MUSCLE MEMORY EXERCISES
UTILISING THE CHROMATIC SCALE.

Table of Contents.

Table of Contents.

Foreward

Daily Warm Ups for Bass Guitar.

Bass Guitar Method for developing a dedicated daily practice routine utilising scales, modes & arpeggios.

One of the most important aspects of learning any instrument is being able to set aside time to practice. Even if you have only 30 min per day, by organising your time and having the dedication to follow through with your plan, progress is yours to be had.
All exercises in this book are given in bass tab and bass clef enabling bass players of all levels and musical backgrounds to have access to musical exercises that help to build instrumental facility and musicianship.
Have the dedication to practice the exercises slowly, working on good time, tone and intonation.
As a wise instructor once said to me " there's no magic powder ".
Great players worked hard to get there, if it is your wish and your intention, you can get there too.

All exercises are provided in 12 keys. For the advanced student, practice the book in 12 keys, for the beginning to intermediate student practice the exercises in one key to gain familiarity with the instrument. When the exercises become comfortable move to another key until all keys are comfortable.

Scale studies are designed to help the bassist to learn the fingerboard while building dexterity, flexibilty, stamina as well as building muscle memory and training the ear.

The exercises in this book are practiced by professional musicians of all backgrounds , from rock to jazz to classiscal musicians.

Part 1   FINGER CO ORDINATION AND MUSCLE MEMORY EXERCISES
                UTILISING THE CHROMATIC SCALE

The first series of exercises in this book are dedicated to establishing coordination between the left and right hand and making the student aware of their own muscle memory.

The exercises outline the chromatic scale and permutations of the chromatic scale played on all open strings, ascending and descending. The exercises then progress to string crossing exercises across 2 , 3 then 4 strings utilising the chromatic scale played in root 5th , root 5th octave root formation.

Practicing the chromatic scales played in 5ths ascending and descending by a half step or semitone the bassist will have played all notes on the fretboard. This is an important tool for unlocking the fretboard mysteries, enabling the bassist to play in any position and know what notes are under their fingers at all times by using specific anchor points.

The chromatic scale 2 octaves ascending

The chromatic scale 2 octaves descending

Exercise 2   THE CHROMATIC SCALE PLAYED OVER 2 OCTAVES ON 1 STRING *

The chromatic scale played on the E string

The chromatic scale played on the A string

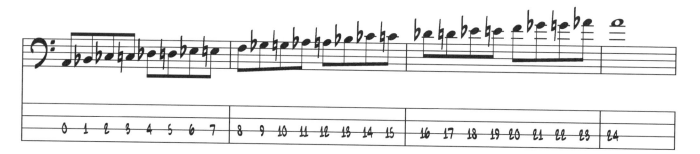

The chromatic scale played on the D string

The chromatic scale played on the G string

Exercise 3   THE CHROMATIC SCALE UTILISING THE ROOT AND THE 5TH
STRING CROSSING OVER 2 STRINGS

The relationship of the root and the 5th is a sound that is heard in all styles of music, the 5th helps to resovle back to the root or tonic. The relationship of the root and the 5th also helps the bassist to know what notes are under their fingers when in various positions on the fretboard.

After playing through the following exercises using the E, A & D strings as anchor points the bassist will be aware that we have covered all the notes on the 4 string bass, by playing the interval of 2 notes eg. Root & 5th.

The chromatic scale exercise utilizing roots and 5ths ascending on the E string

The chromatic scale exercise utilizing roots and 5ths descending on the E string

The chromatic scale exercise utilizing roots and 5ths ascending on the A string

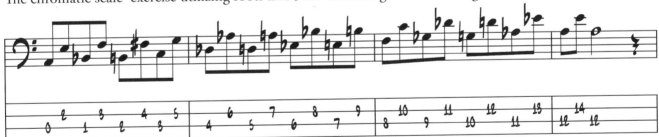

The chromatic scale exercise utilizing roots and 5ths descending on the A string

The chromatic scale exercise utilizing roots and 5ths ascending on the D string

The chromatic scale exercise utilizing roots and 5ths descending on the D string

Exercise 4. THE CHROMATIC SCALE UTILISING THE ROOT, 5TH, OCTAVE & ROOT
STRING CROSSING OVER 3 STRINGS

The relationship of the root, the 5th and the octave now opens up a wider range of melodic choices for the bassist.

After playing through the following exercises using the E & A strings as anchor points the bassist will be aware that we have covered all the notes on the 4 string bass by playing the interval of 3 notes eg. Root & 5th octave.

Exercise on the E string - Root, 5th, octave, root. Ascending

Exercise on the E string - Root, 5th, octave, root. Descending

Exercise on the A String Root, 5th, octave, root. Ascending

Exercise on the A String Root, 5th, octave, root. Descending

Exercise 5. THE CHROMATIC SCALE UTILISING THE ROOT, 5TH, OCTAVE & ROOT
STRING CROSSING OVER 4 STRINGS

Notice this exercise is similar to exercise # 4. The interval of root , 5th, octave, root is played, then crossing to the A string (or move up a 4th) to repeat the interval of root, 5th, octave, root again.

String crossing exercise using the E and A strings as the anchor point.
Root 5th octave utilising string crossing across all strings in position.

To summarize the material in the first chapter, we looked at the use of the chromatic scale to build left and right hand co-ordination and to become aware of the benefits of muscle memory.

By applying the intervallic exercises to the ascending and descending chromatic scales on the E, A, D & G strings, the bassist has now covered every note on the fretboard. The mysteries of the fretboard are becoming unlocked.

Investing a small amount of the daily practice routine to the exercises in chapter 1 will help the bassist of all levels to develop a solid grounding in rudiments therefore enabling a solid foundation in bass fundamentals.

Practice all exercises in the book slowly striving for even sound and tone across all strings and all notes.
Practice with a metronome.
The exercises in the book are mostly written as 8th notes.
All exercises can be played as whole notes, qarter notes, 16th notes, etc.

When playing the exercises with a metronome, strive for good tone, good time and most importantly give every note its full rhythmic value. eg. If playing quarter notes let every note sound for the full quarter note value. Dont clip the notes, when you are first developing your hand strength some of the exercises are difficult to obtain even sound across all notes, especially on the string crossing exercises.

Play the exercises SLOWLY and give yourself time to develop a sound. Then increase the tempo.
These exercises alone will make dramatic shifts in youre tone, articulation, time, as well as left & right hand coordination and muscle memory.

The book is not about playing the exercises as fast as you can. Its about developing a solid foundation in rudiments and being aware of where you are and what youre doing.

When you can get there and then forget about it, thats when the true magic of music takes over.

Enjoy the gifts of music.

Part 2.   SCALE STUDIES IN THE MAJOR KEYS

The following exercises in Part 2 of the book expand on the development of muscle memory, co-ordination, fretboard knowledge and tone production.

The exercises outline the Major keys and the related arpeggios and modes built from the Major scale as well as sequences and drills used by professional musicians of all styles.

All exercises are taken through all twelve keys to enable the student to develop true freedom on the instrument by devoting a small amount of their daily practice routine to the bass rudiments in this book.

It is recommended to start in the key of C and work through the book in a stepwise manner. Become familiar with the exercise before moving onto the next exercise, when the exercises are comfortable in one key and tone production and time keeping are consistant move onto the next key.

SCALE STUDIES IN THE KEY OF C MAJOR

C major scale 2 octaves

C major 7 arpeggio 2 octaves

D Dorian scale 2 octaves

D min 7 arpeggio 2 octaves

E Phrygian scale

E min 7 arpeggio

F Lydian scale

F maj 7 arpeggio

G Mixolydian scale

G 7 arpeggio

A Aeolian scale

A min7 arpeggio

B Locrian scale

B min7 b5 arpeggio

4 Note Scale Groupings

The following exercise outlines the use of 4 note groupings moving stepwise diatonically through the scale of C major.

For example, the 4 note grouping starts on the root note or 1st degree of the scale and progresses stepwise. The exercise then descends from the 2nd octave C back to the root.

Ascending

Descending

Permutation 2   Up & Down

As in the previous exercise the following exercise outlines the use of 4 note groupings moving stepwise diatonically through the scale of C major.

Notice in exercise #2 the 4 note grouping starts on the root note or 1st degree of the scale and progresses stepwise. In this example we descend when we hit the 5th note in the sequence eg. descending from the 2nd 4 note grouping.

Ascending

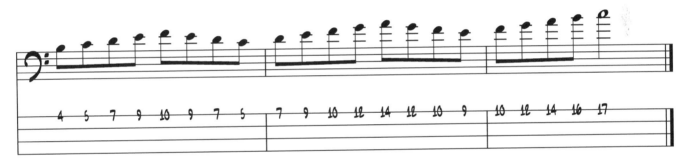

Descending

BROKEN THIRDS

Ascending

Descending

4 Note groupings Diatonic Triads

Ascending 1351

Descending 1351

Ascending 1531

Descending 1531

4 note groupings Diatonic 7th Chords

Ascending

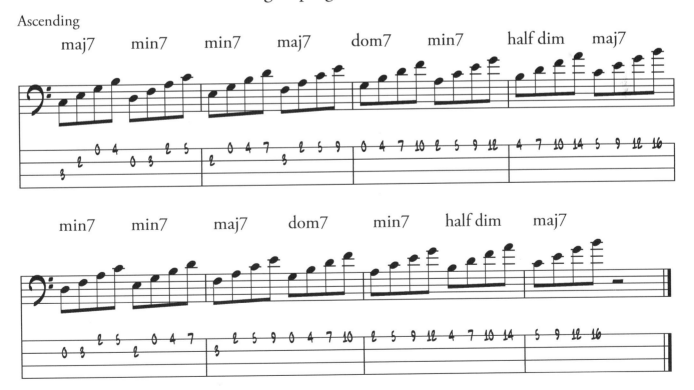

Descending

4 note groupings Diatonic 7th Chords

Permutation 2
Ascending & descending

Permutation 3
Down the chord stepwise up the scale

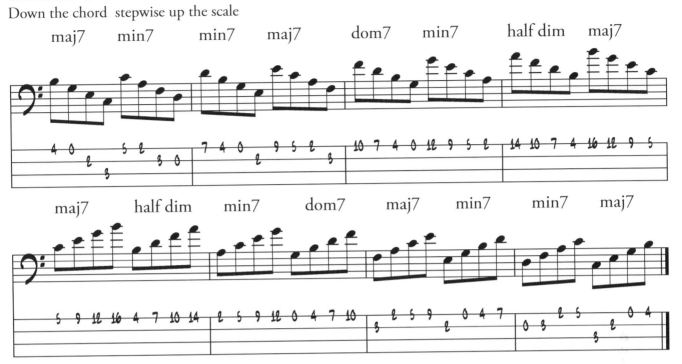

3 Note Groupings

C major scale in triplet groupings
Ascending

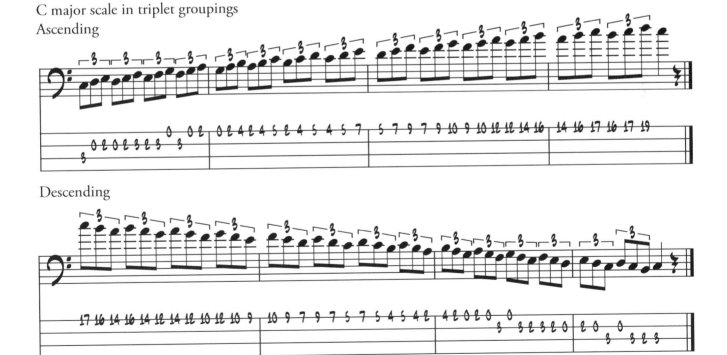

Descending

Diatonic 7th Chords in Triplets

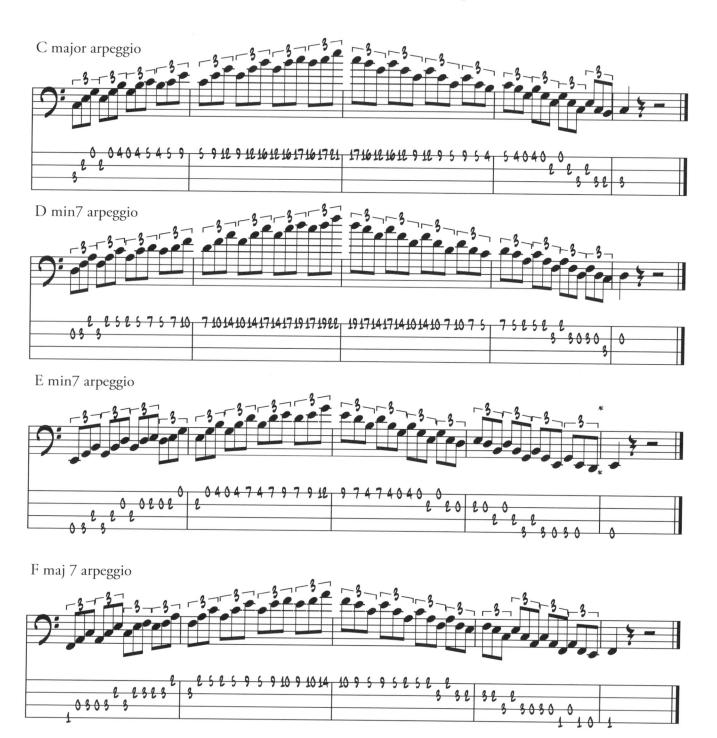

C major arpeggio

D min7 arpeggio

E min7 arpeggio

F maj 7 arpeggio

*The D natural in this exercise is out of the range of the 4 string bass. This passage can be played 8va eg. 1 octave higher than written.

G 7 arpeggio

A min7 arpeggio

B min7 b5 arpeggio

C major arpeggio

Scale studies in the key of Db Major

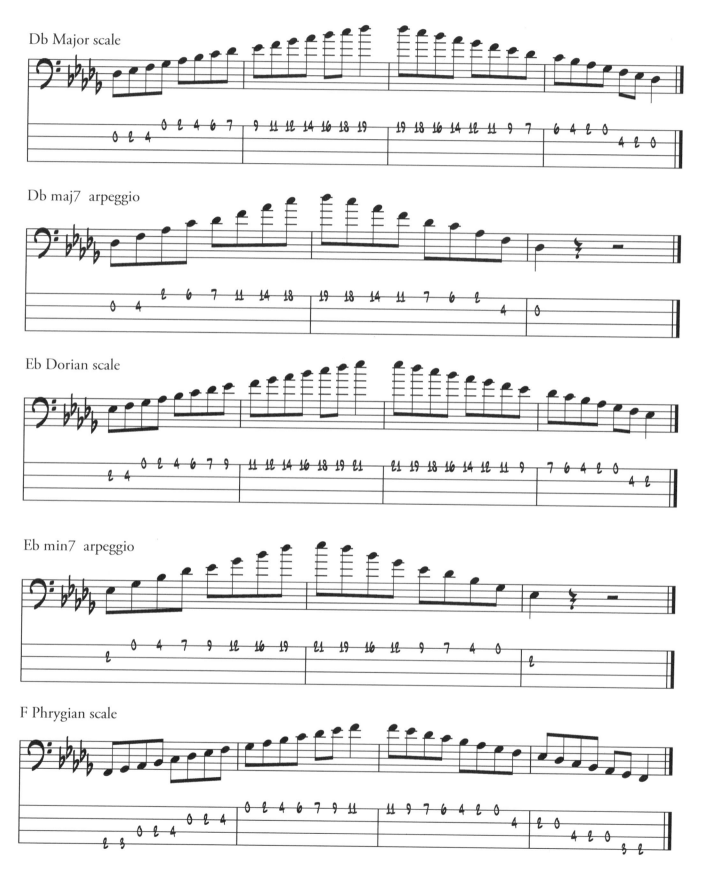

F min7 arpeggio

Gb Lydian scale

Gb maj7   arpeggio

Ab Mixolydian scale

Ab7 arpeggio

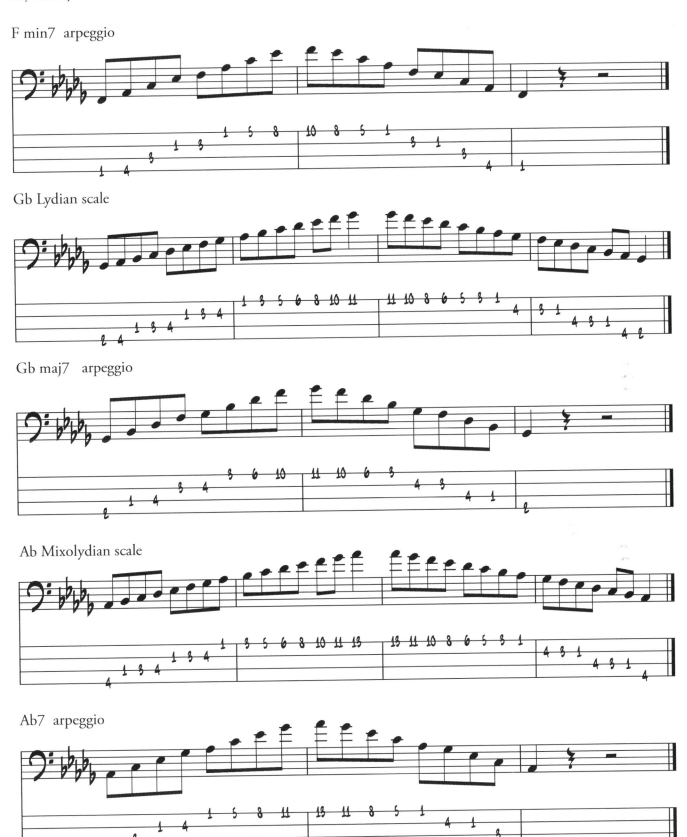

Bb Aeolian scale

Bb min7 arpeggio

C Locrian scale

C min7 b5 arpeggio

4 Note Scale Groupings

The following exercise outlines the use of 4 note groupings moving stepwise diatonically through the scale of Db major.

For example, the 4 note grouping starts on the root note or 1st degree of the scale and progresses stepwise. The exercise then descends from the 2nd octave Db back to the root.

Ascending

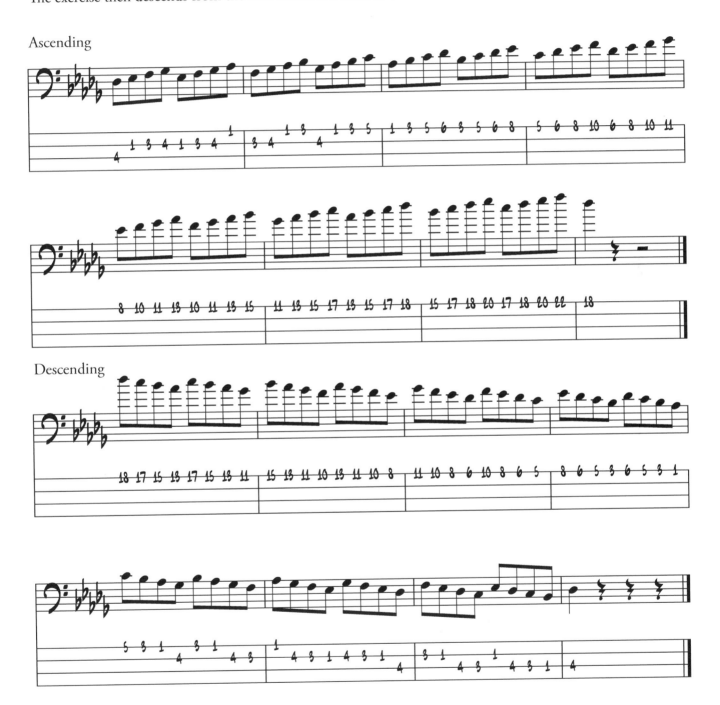

Descending

Permutation 2   Up & Down

As in the previous exercise the following exercise outlines the use of 4 note groupings moving stepwise diatonically through the scale of Db major.
Notice in exercise #2 the 4 note grouping starts on the root note or 1st degree of the scale and progresses stepwise. In this example we descend when we hit the 5th note in the sequence eg. descending from the 2nd 4 note grouping.

Ascending

Descending

Broken Thirds

Ascending

Descending

4 Note Groupings Diatonic Triads

Ascending 1351

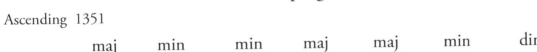

Descending 1351

Ascending 1531

Descending 1531

4 note groupings Diatonic 7th Chords

Ascending

Descending

Permutation 2
Ascending & descending

Permutation 3
Down the chord stepwise up the scale

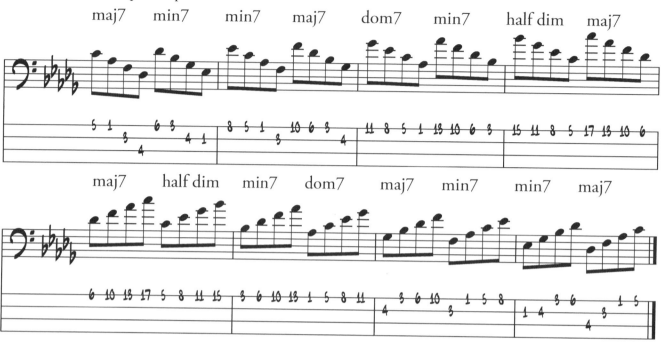

3 Note Groupings

Db major scale in triplet groupings
Ascending

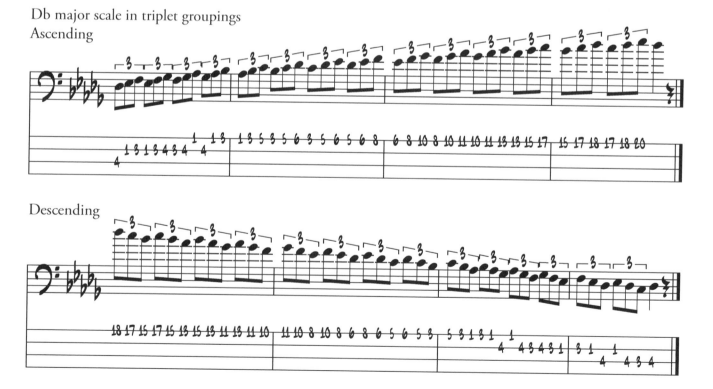

Descending

Diatonic 7th Chords in Triplets

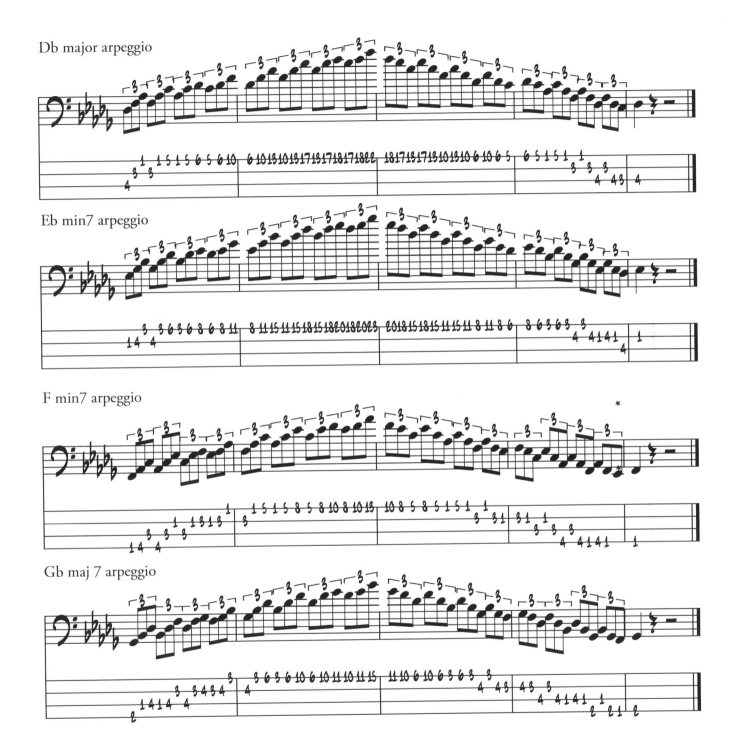

Db major arpeggio

Eb min7 arpeggio

F min7 arpeggio

Gb maj 7 arpeggio

* The low Eb in this exercise is out of the range of the 4 string bass. This passage can
be played 8va eg. 1 octave higher than written.

Ab 7 arpeggio

Bb min7 arpeggio

C min7 b5 arpeggio

Db major arpeggio

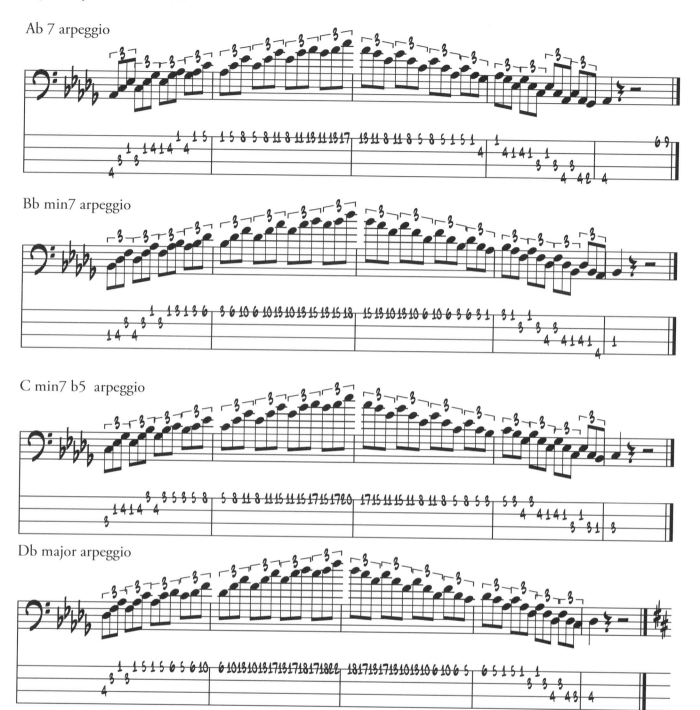

Scale studies in the key of D Major

Scales, Modes and Arpeggios over 2 octaves

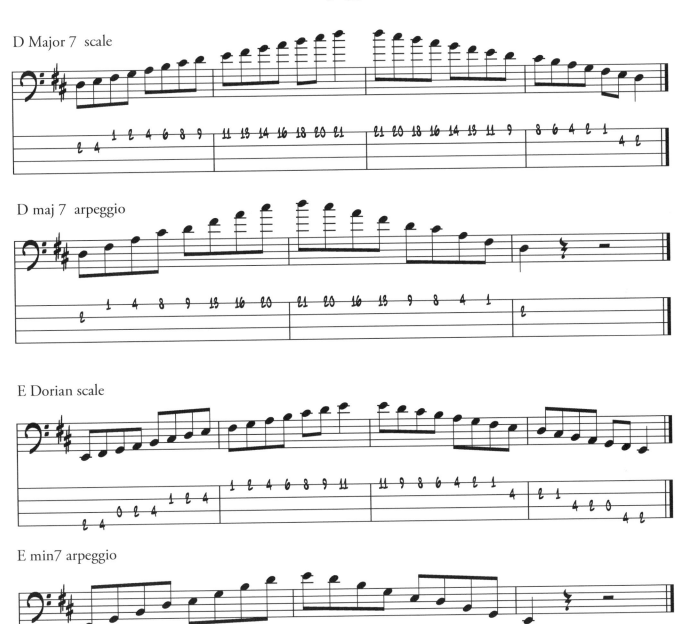

D Major 7 scale

D maj 7 arpeggio

E Dorian scale

E min7 arpeggio

F# Phrygian scale

F# min7 arpeggio

G Lydian scale

G maj 7 arpeggio

A Mixolydian scale

A dom7 arpeggio

B Aeolian scale

B min7 arpeggio

C# Locrian scale

C# min7 b5 arpeggio

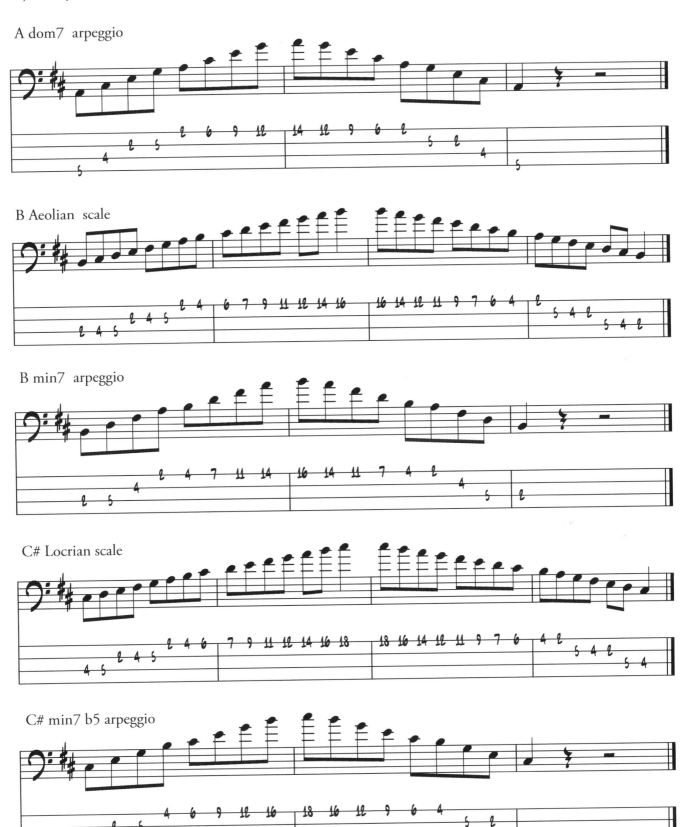

4 Note Scale Groupings

The following exercise outlines the use of 4 note groupings moving stepwise diatonically through the scale of D major.

For example, the 4 note grouping starts on the root note or 1st degree of the scale and progresses stepwise. The exercise then descends from the 2nd octave D back to the root.

Ascending

Descending

Permutation 2   Up & Down

As in the previous exercise the following exercise outlines the use of 4 note groupings moving stepwise diatonically through the scale of D major.

Notice in exercise #2 the 4 note grouping starts on the root note or 1st degree of the scale and progresses stepwise. In this example we descend when we hit the 5th note in the sequence eg. descending from the 2nd 4 note grouping.

Ascending

Descending

Broken Thirds

Ascending

Descending

4 Note Groupings Diatonic Triads

Ascending 1351

Descending 1351

Ascending 1531

Descending 1531

4 Note Groupings Diatonic 7th chords

Ascending

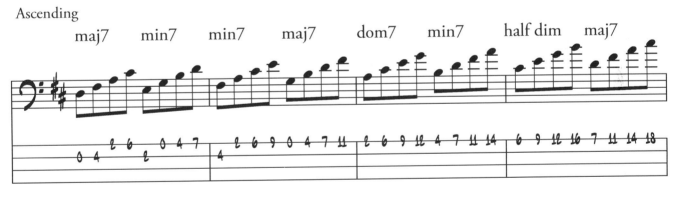

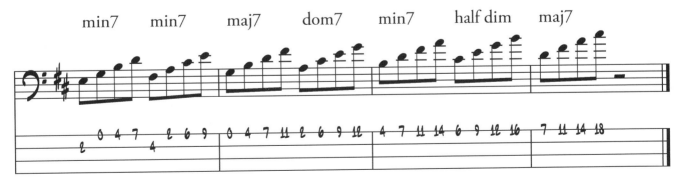

Descending

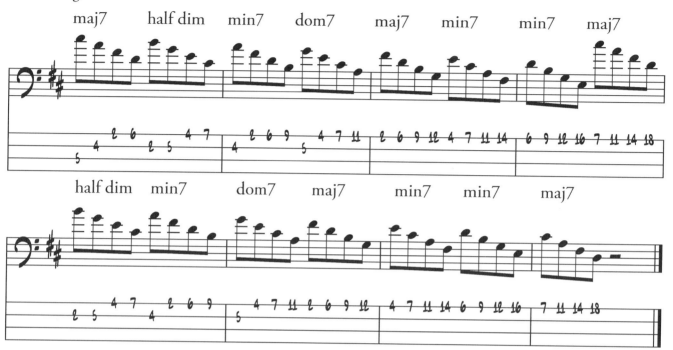

Permutation 2
Ascending & descending

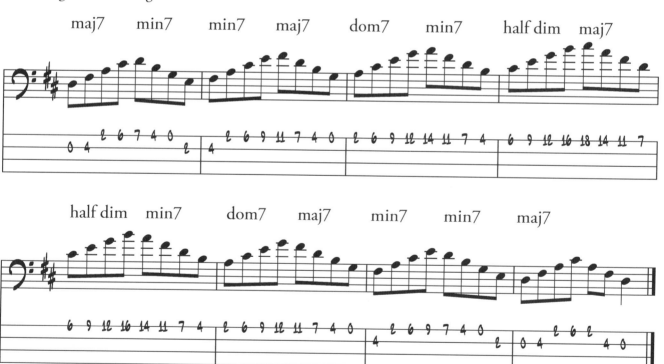

Permutation 3
Down the chord stepwise up the scale

3 Note Groupings

D major scale in triplet groupings
Ascending

Descending

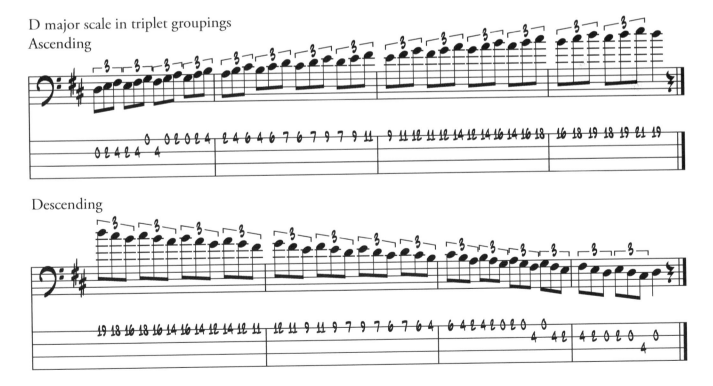

Diatonic 7th Chords in Triplets

D maj arpeggio

E min7 arpeggio

F# min7 arpeggio

G maj 7 arpeggio

A 7 arpeggio

B min7 arpeggio

C# min7 b5 arpeggio

D major arpeggio

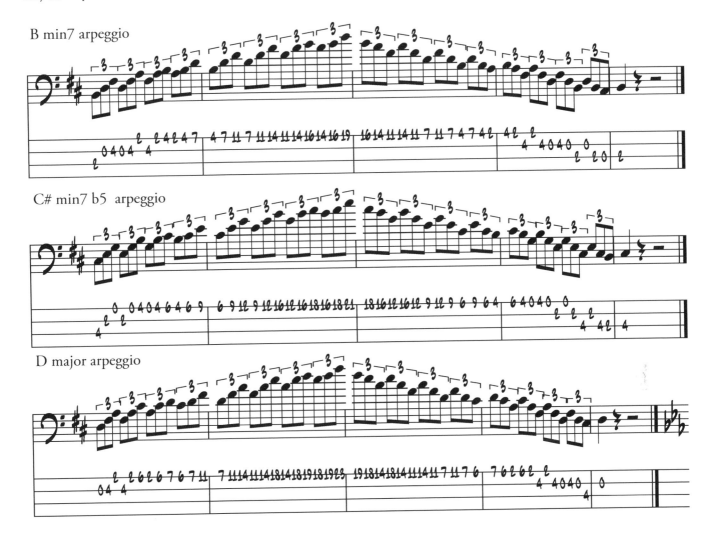

Scale studies in the key of Eb Major

Scales, Modes and Arpeggios over 2 octaves

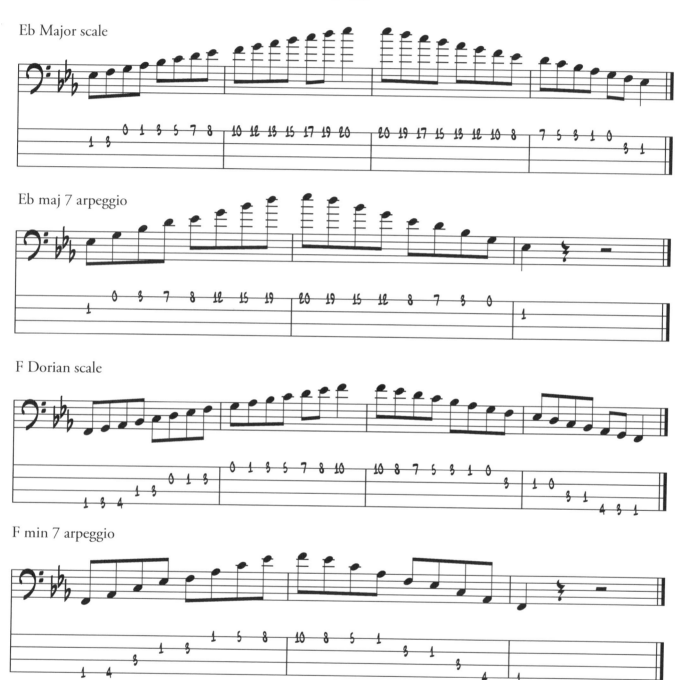

Eb Major scale

Eb maj 7 arpeggio

F Dorian scale

F min 7 arpeggio

G Phrygian scale

G min 7 arpeggio

Ab Lydian scale

Ab maj 7 arpeggio

Bb Mixolydian scale

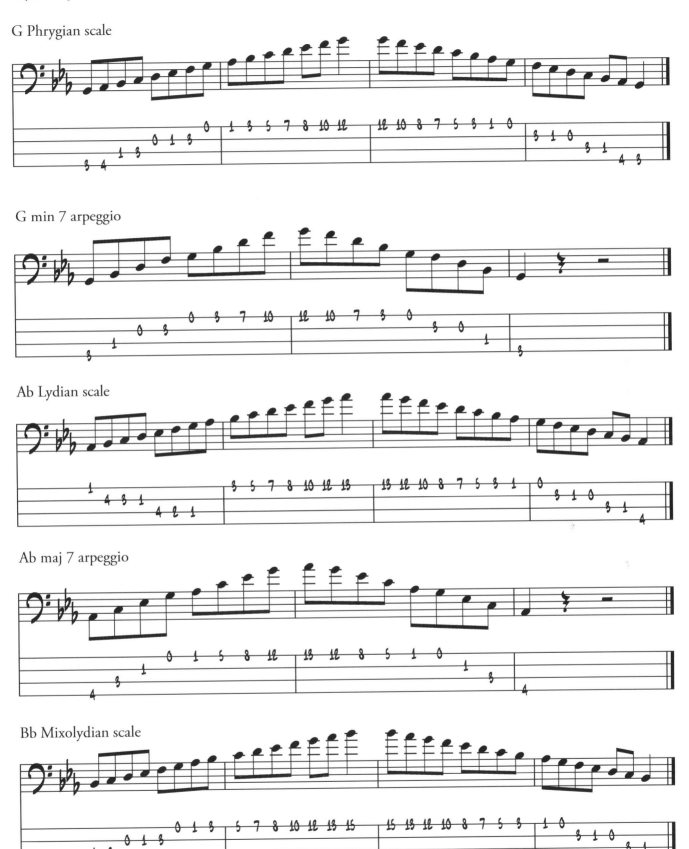

Bb7 arpeggio

C Aeolian scale

C min7 arpeggio

D Locrian scale

D min7 b5 arpeggio

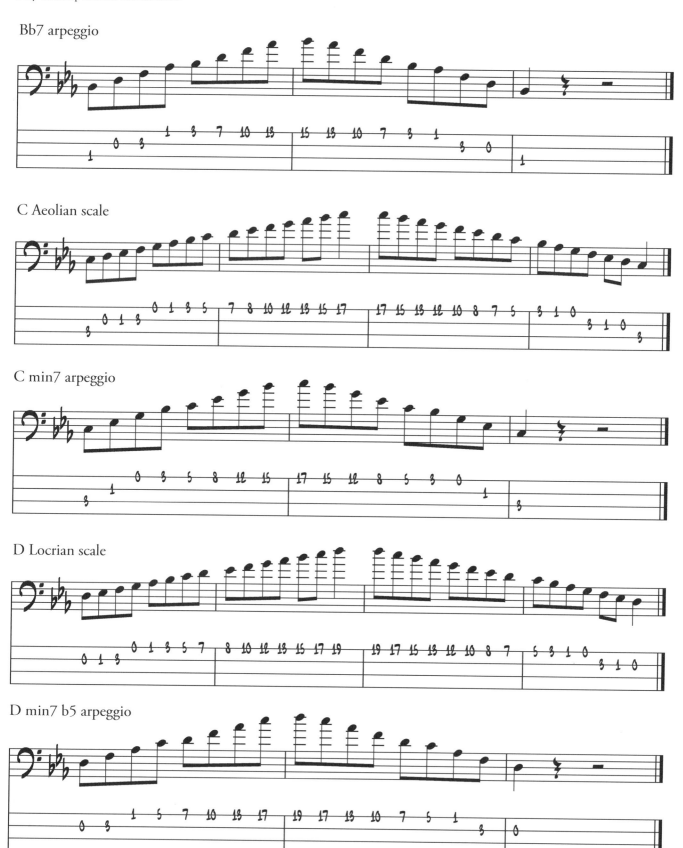

4 Note Scale Groupings

The following exercise outlines the use of 4 note groupings moving stepwise diatonically through the scale of Eb major.

For example, the 4 note grouping starts on the root note or 1st degree of the scale and progresses stepwise. The exercise then descends from the 2nd octave Eb back to the root.

Ascending

Descending

Permutation 2   Up & Down

As in the previous exercise the following exercise outlines the use of 4 note groupings moving stepwise diatonically through the scale of Eb major.

Notice in exercise #2 the 4 note grouping starts on the root note or 1st degree of the scale and progresses stepwise. In this example we descend when we hit the 5th note in the sequence eg. descending from the 2nd 4 note grouping.

Ascending

Descending

Broken Thirds

Ascending

Descending

Descending

4 Note Groupings Diatonic Triads

Ascending 1351

Descending 1351

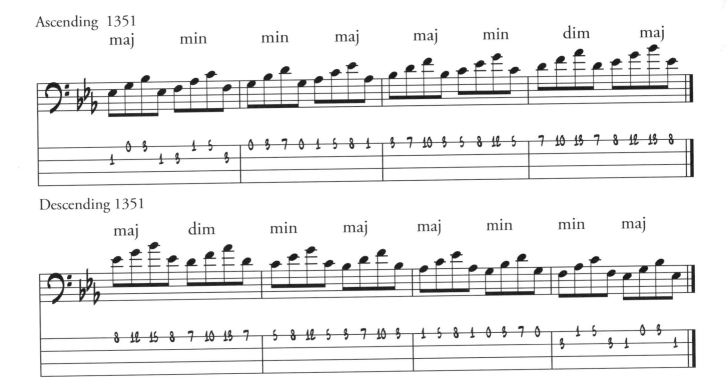

Ascending 1531

Descending 1531

4 Note Groupings Diatonic 7th Chords

Ascending

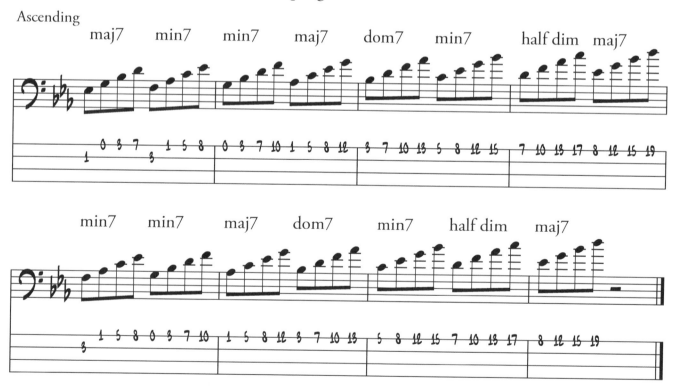

Descending

Permutation 2
Ascending & descending

Permutation 3
Down the chord stepwise up the scale

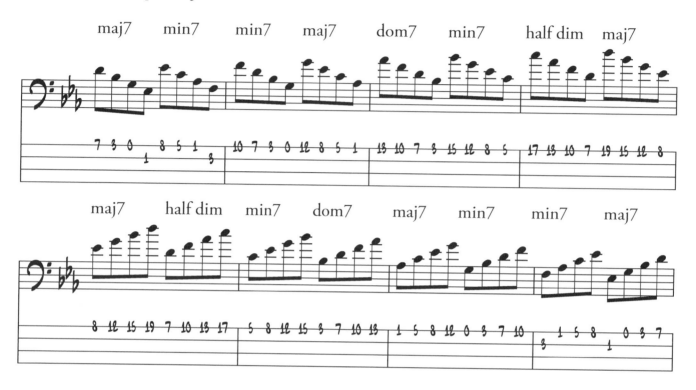

3 Note Groupings

Eb major scale in triplet groupings
Ascending

Descending

Diatonic 7th Chords in Triplets

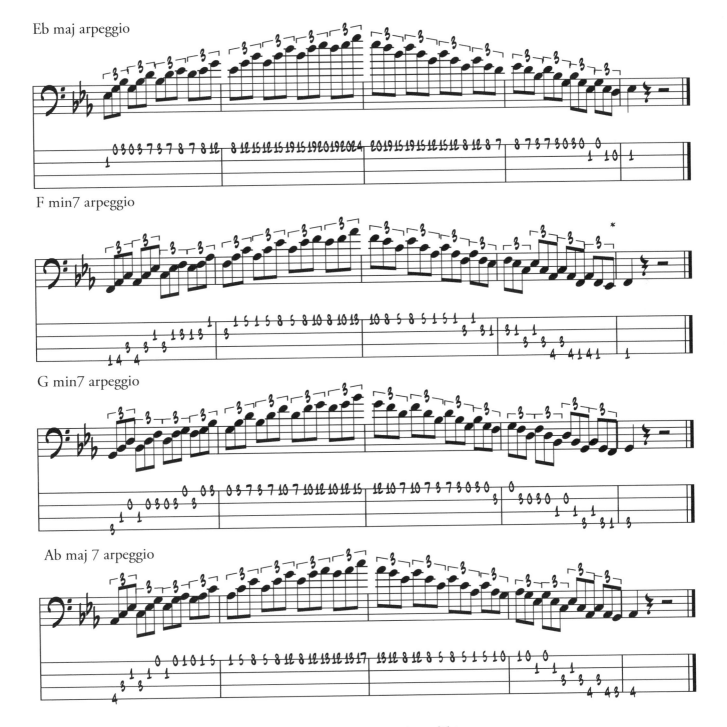

*The Eb in this exercise is out of the range of the 4 string bass. This passage can be played 8va eg. 1 octave higher than written.

Bb 7 arpeggio

C min7 arpeggio

D min7 b5 arpeggio

Eb maj arpeggio

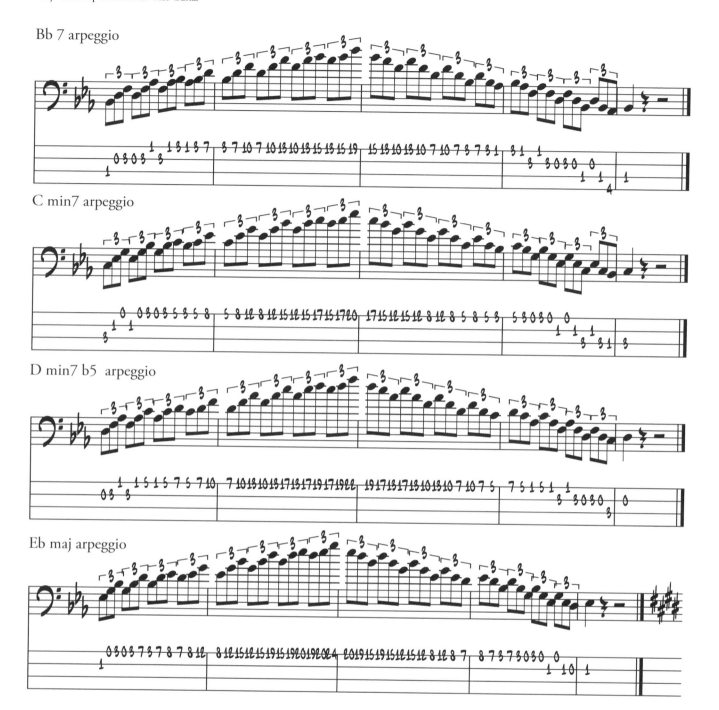

Scale studies in the key of E Major

Scales, Modes and Arpeggios over 2 octaves

E Major scale

E maj 7 arpeggio

F# Dorian scale

F# min 7 arpeggio

G# Phrygian scale

G# min 7 arpeggio

A Lydian scale

Amaj 7 arpeggio

B Mixolydian scale

B 7 arpeggio

C# Aeolian scale

C# min7 arpeggio

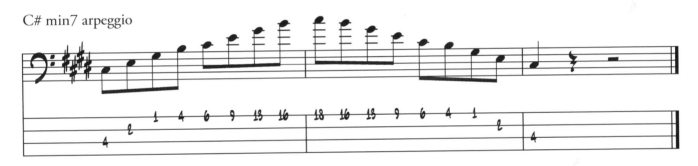

D# Locrian scale

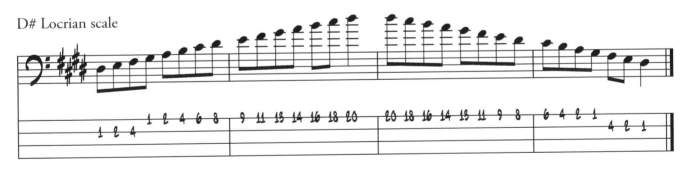

D# min7 b5 arpeggio

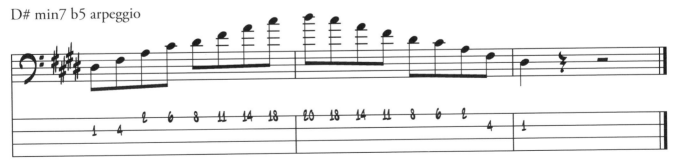

4 Note Scale Groupings

The following exercise outlines the use of 4 note groupings moving stepwise diatonically through the scale of E major.

For example, the 4 note grouping starts on the root note or 1st degree of the scale and progresses stepwise. The exercise then descends from the 2nd octave E back to the root.

Ascending

Descending

Permutation 2

Up & Down

As in the previous exercise the following exercise outlines the use of 4 note groupings moving stepwise diatonically through the scale of E major.

Notice in exercise #2 the 4 note grouping starts on the root note or 1st degree of the scale and progresses stepwise. In this example we descend when we hit the 5th note in the sequence eg. descending from the 2nd 4 note grouping.

Ascending

Descending

Broken Thirds

Ascending

Descending

4 Note Groupings Diatonic Triads

Ascending 1351

maj   min   min   maj   maj   min   dim   maj

Descending 1351

maj   dim   min   maj   maj   min   min   maj

Ascending 1531

maj · min · min · maj · maj · min · dim · maj

Descending 1531

maj · dim · min · maj · maj · min · min · maj

4 Note Groupings Diatonic 7th Chords

Ascending

maj7 · min7 · min7 · maj7 · dom7 · min7 · half dim · maj7

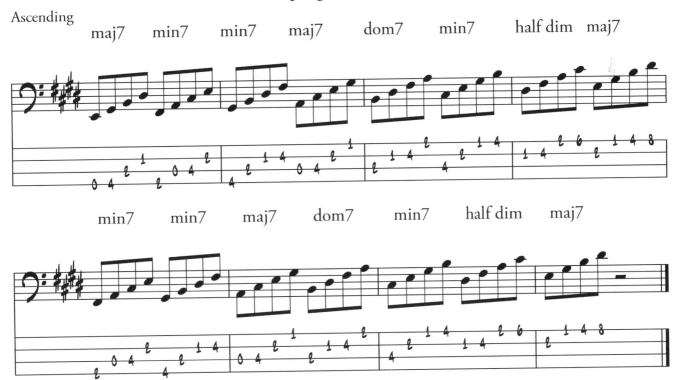

min7 · min7 · maj7 · dom7 · min7 · half dim · maj7

Descending

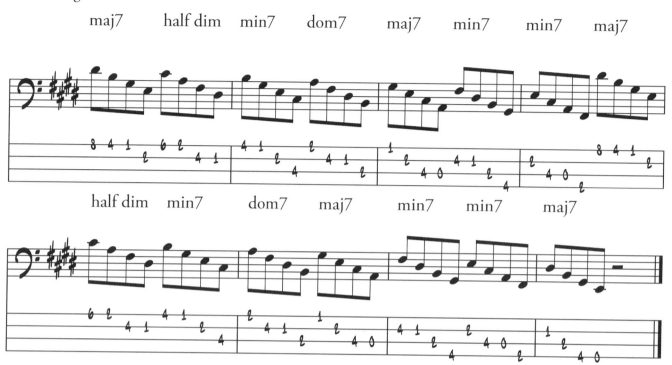

Ascending & descending

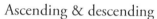

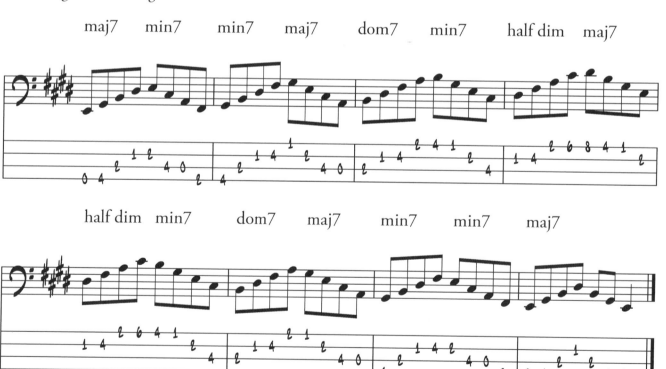

Permutation 3
Down the chord stepwise up the scale

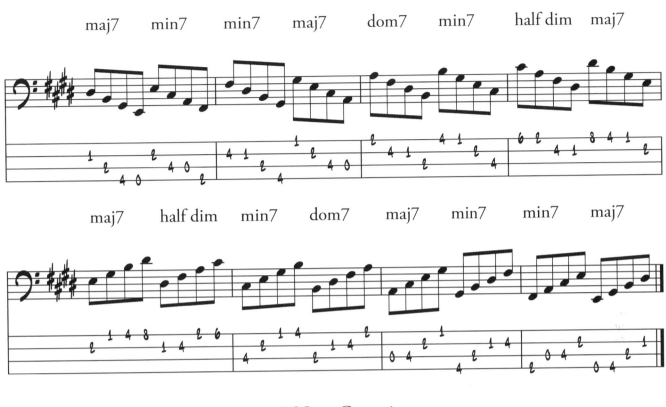

3 Note Groupings

E major scale in triplet groupings
Ascending

Descending

Diatonic 7th Chords in Triplets

E maj arpeggio

F# min7 arpeggio

G# min7 arpeggio

A maj 7 arpeggio

*The D# in this exercise is out of the range of the 4 string. This passage can
be played 8va eg. 1 octave higher than written.

B 7 arpeggio

C# min7 arpeggio

D# min7 b5 arpeggio

E maj arpeggio

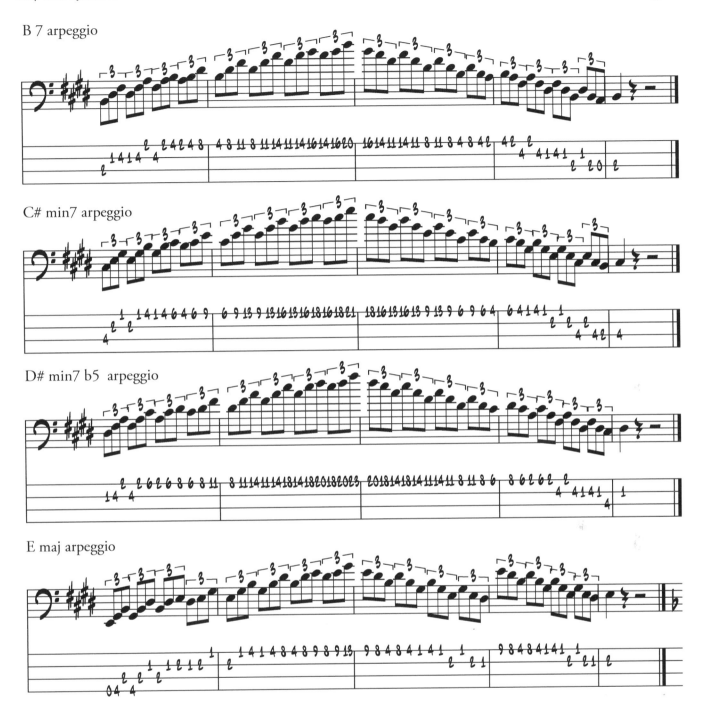

Scale studies in the key of F Major

Scales, Modes and Arpeggios over 2 octaves

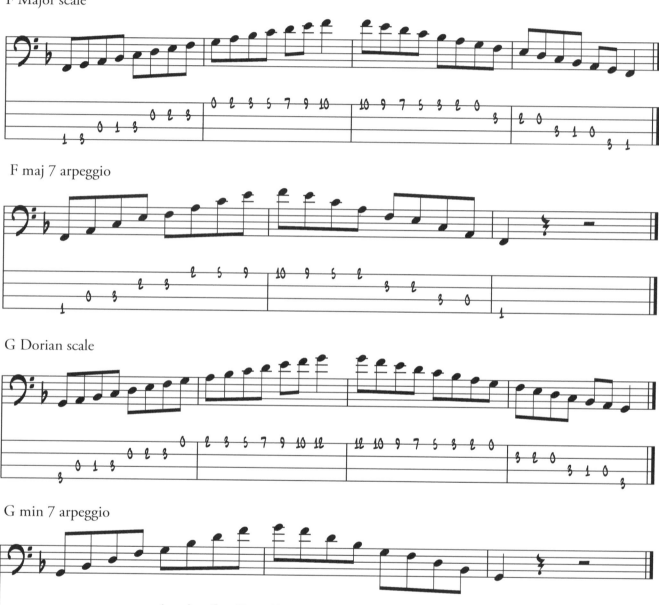

F Major scale

F maj 7 arpeggio

G Dorian scale

G min 7 arpeggio

A Phrygian scale

A min 7 arpeggio

Bb Lydian scale

Bb maj 7 arpeggio

C Mixolydian scale

C 7 arpeggio

D Aeolian scale

D min7 arpeggio

E Locrian scale

E min7 b5 arpeggio

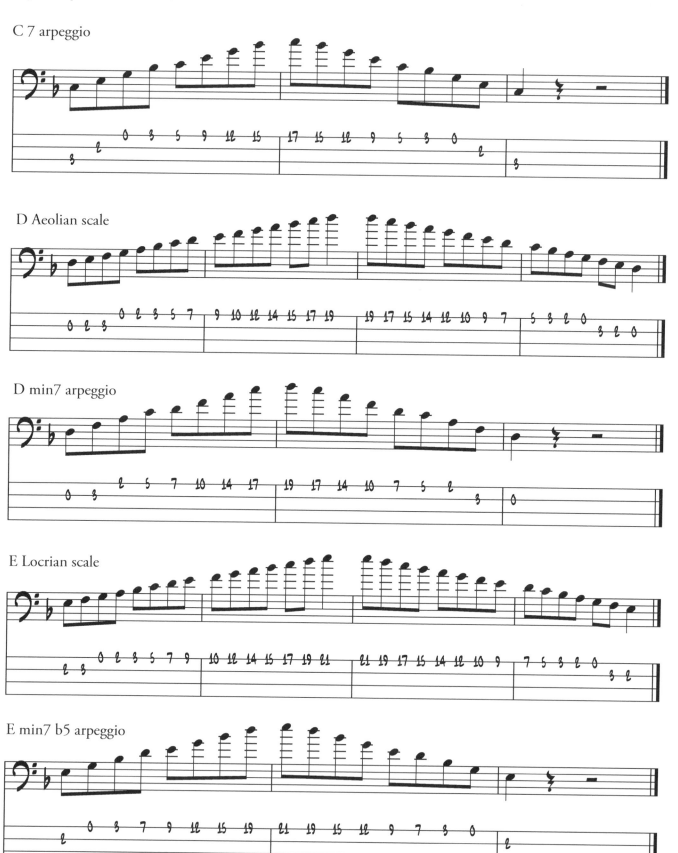

4 Note Scale Groupings

The following exercise outlines the use of 4 note groupings moving stepwise diatonically through the scale of F major.

For example, the 4 note grouping starts on the root note or 1st degree of the scale and progresses stepwise. The exercise then descends from the 2nd octave F back to the root.

Ascending

Descending

* The D in this exercise is out of the range of the 4 string bass . This passage can be played 8va eg. 1 octave higher than written.

Permutation 2

Up & Down

As in the previous exercise the following exercise outlines the use of 4 note groupings moving stepwise diatonically through the scale of F major.

Notice in exercise #2 the 4 note grouping starts on the root note or 1st degree of the scale and progresses stepwise. In this example we descend when we hit the 5th note in the sequence eg. descending from the 2nd 4 note grouping.

Ascending

Descending

Broken Thirds

Ascending

Descending

4 Note Groupings Diatonic Triads

Ascending 1351

Descending 1351

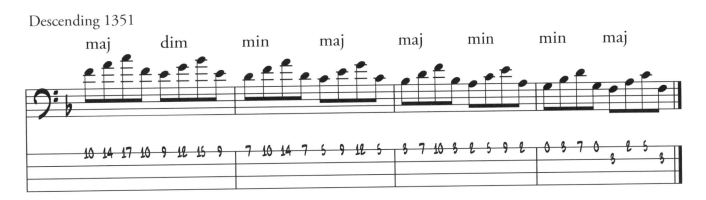

Ascending 1531

Descending 1531

4 Note Groupings Diatonic 7th Chords

Ascending

Descending

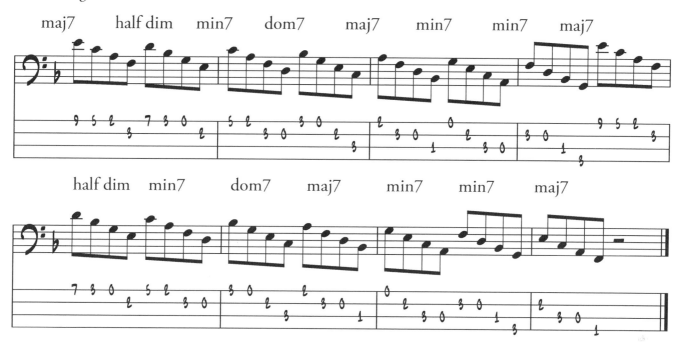

Permutation 2
Ascending & descending

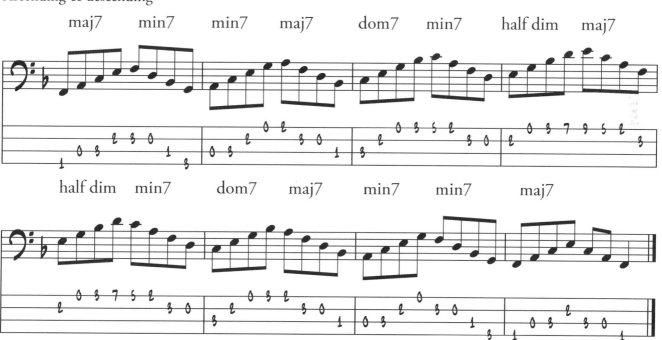

Permutation 3
Down the chord stepwise up the scale

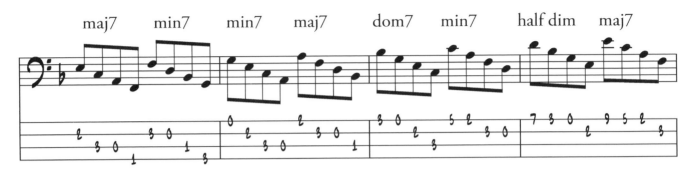

3 Note Groupings

F major scale in triplet groupings
Ascending

Descending

Diatonic 7th Chords in Triplets

F maj arpeggio

G min7 arpeggio

A min7 arpeggio

Bb maj 7 arpeggio

C 7 arpeggio

D min7 arpeggio

E min7 b5 arpeggio

F major arpeggio

Scale studies in the key of F# Major

Scales, Modes and Arpeggios over 2 octaves

F# Major scale

F# maj 7 arpeggio

G# Dorian scale

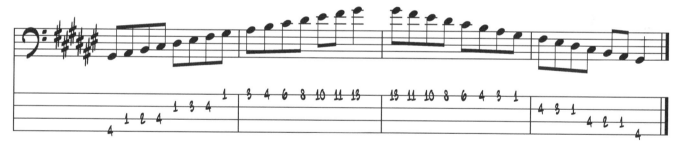

G# min 7 arpeggio

A# Phrygian scale

A# min 7 arpeggio

B Lydian scale

B major 7 arpeggio

C# Mixolydian scale

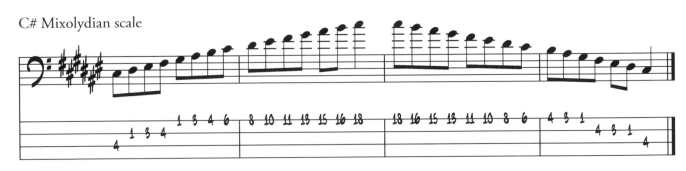

C# 7 arpeggio

D# Aeolian scale

D# min7 arpeggio

E# Locrian scale

E# min7 b5 arpeggio

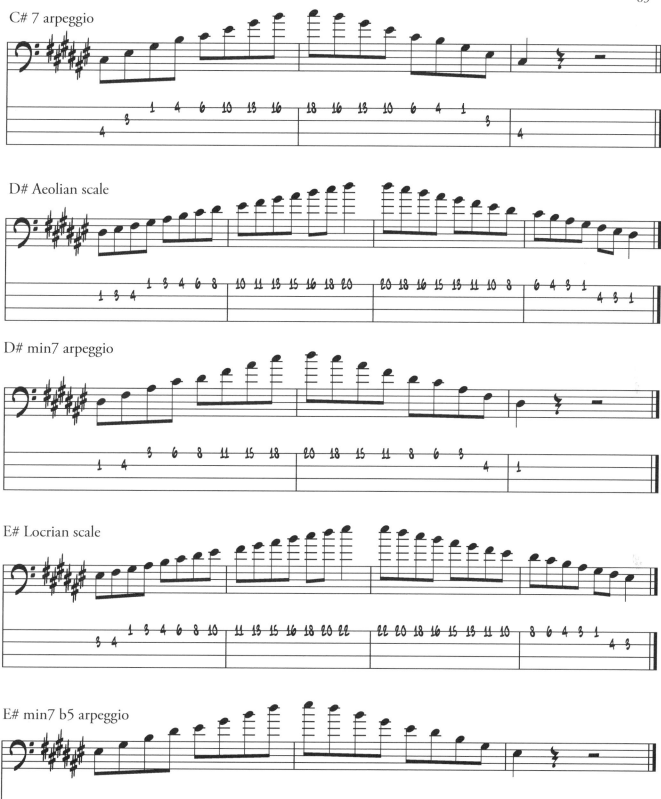

4 Note Scale Groupings

The following exercise outlines the use of 4 note groupings moving stepwise diatonically through the scale of F# major.

For example, the 4 note grouping starts on the root note or 1st degree of the scale and progresses stepwise. The exercise then descends from the 2nd octave F# back to the root.

Ascending

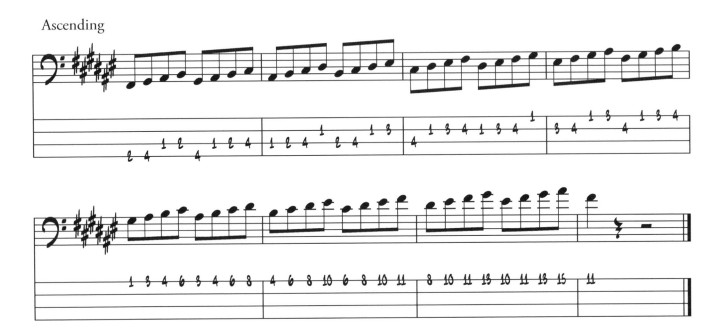

Descending

* The D# in this exercise is out of the range of the 4 string bass . This passage can be played 8va eg. 1 octave higher than written.

Permutation #2   Up & Down

As in the previous exercise the following exercise outlines the use of 4 note groupings moving stepwise diatonically through the scale of F# major.

Notice in exercise #2 the 4 note grouping starts on the root note or 1st degree of the scale and progresses stepwise. In this example we descend when we hit the 5th note in the sequence eg. descending from the 2nd 4 note grouping.

Ascending

Descending

* The D# in this exercise is out of the range of the 4 string bass. This passage can be played 8va eg. 1 octave higher than written.

Broken Thirds

Ascending

Descending

4 Note Groupings Diatonic Triads

Ascending 1351

maj   min   min   maj   maj   min   dim   maj

Descending 1351

maj   dim   min   maj   maj   min   min   maj

Ascending 1531

Descending 1531

4 Note Groupings Diatonic 7th Chords

Ascending

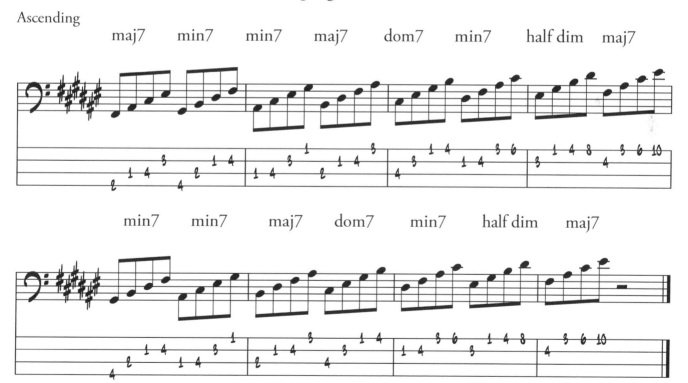

Descending

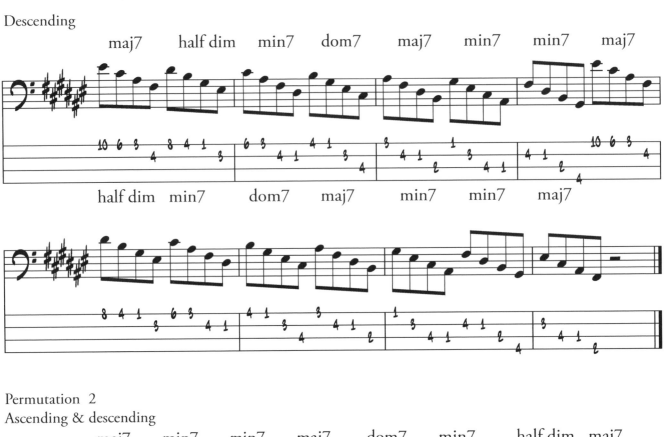

Permutation 2
Ascending & descending

Permutation 3
Down the chord stepwise up the scale

3 Note Groupings

F# major scale in triplet groupings
Ascending

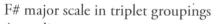

Descending

Diatonic 7th Chords in Ttriplets

F# maj arpeggio

G# min7 arpeggio

A# min7 arpeggio

B maj 7 arpeggio

C# 7 arpeggio

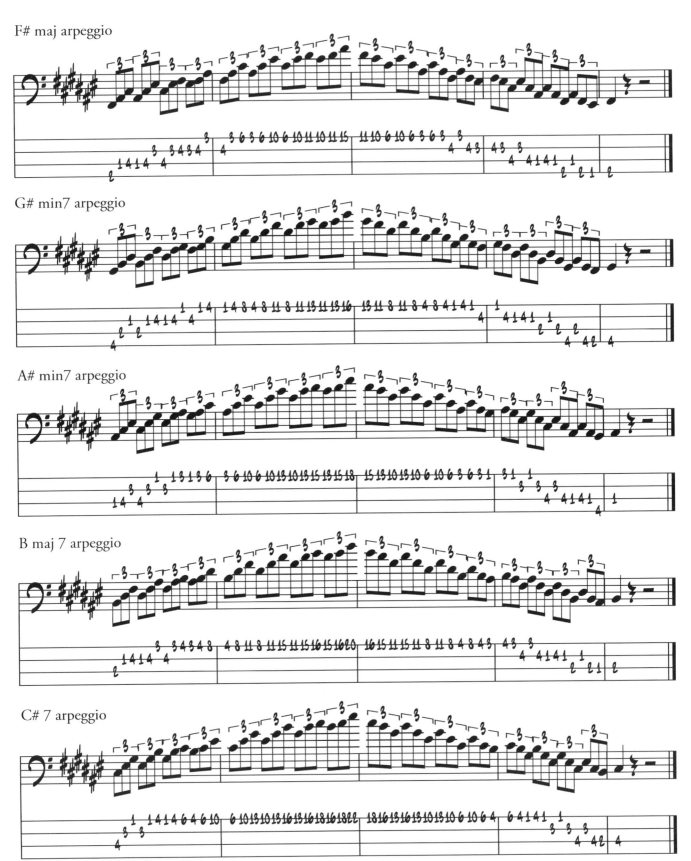

D# min7 arpeggio

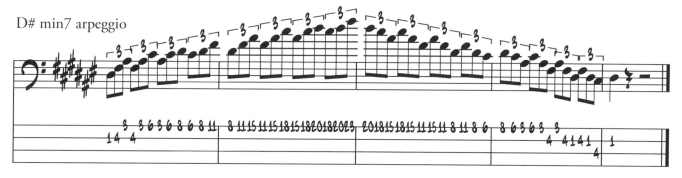

E# min7 b5 arpeggio

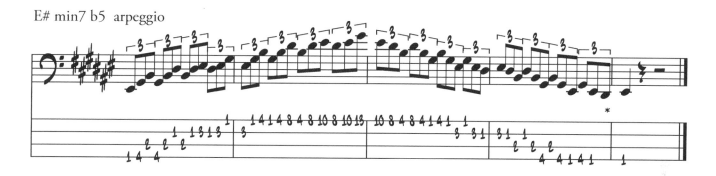

F# maj arpeggio

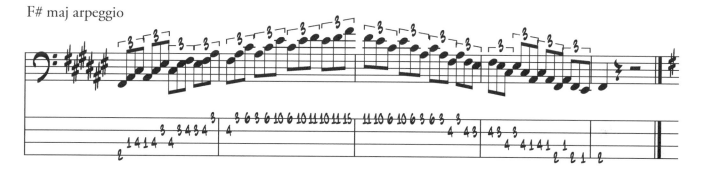

* The D# in this exercise is out of the range of the 4 string bass. This passage can
be played 8va eg. 1 octave higher than written

Scale studies in the key of G Major

Scales, Modes and Arpeggios over 2 octaves

G Major scale

G maj 7 arpeggio

A Dorian scale

A min 7 arpeggio

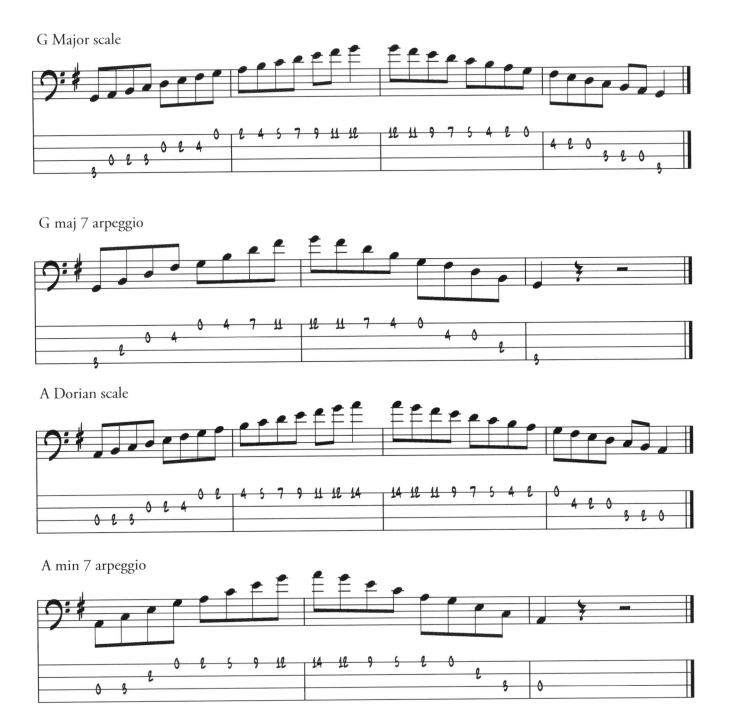

B Phrygian scale

B min 7 arpeggio

C Lydian scale

C maj 7 arpeggio

D Mixolydian scale

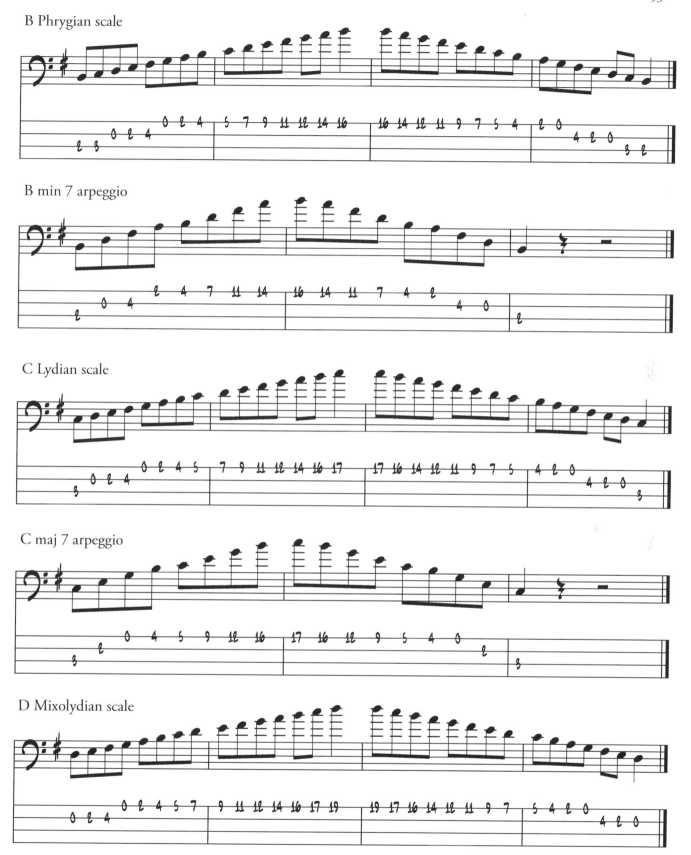

D 7 arpeggio

E Aeolian scale

E min7 arpeggio

F# Locrian scale

F# min7 b5 arpeggio

4 Note Scale Groupings

The following exercise outlines the use of 4 note groupings moving stepwise diatonically through the scale of G major.

For example, the 4 note grouping starts on the root note or 1st degree of the scale and progresses stepwise. The exercise then descends from the 2nd octave G back to the root.

Ascending

Descending

Permutation 2

Up & Down

As in the previous exercise the following exercise outlines the use of 4 note groupings moving stepwise diatonically through the scale of G major.

Notice in exercise #2 the 4 note grouping starts on the root note or 1st degree of the scale and progresses stepwise. In this example we descend when we hit the 5th note in the sequence eg. descending from the 2nd 4 note grouping.

Ascending

Descending

Broken Thirds

Ascending

Descending

4 Note Groupings Diatonic Triads

Ascending 1351

Descending 1351

Ascending 1531

Descending 1531

4 Note Groupings Diatonic 7th Chords

Ascending

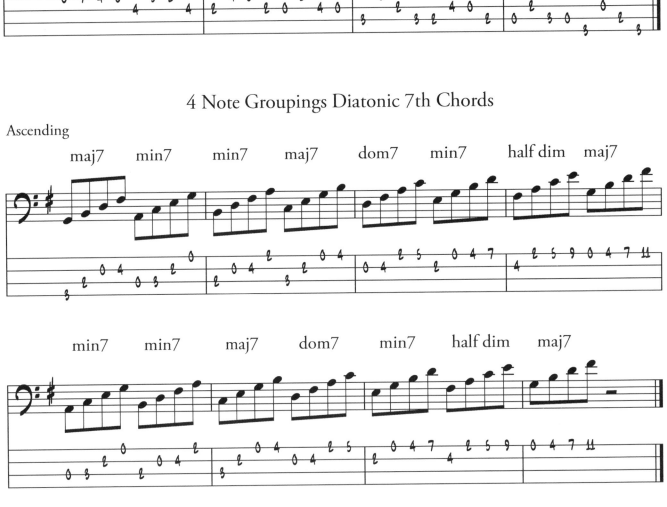

Descending

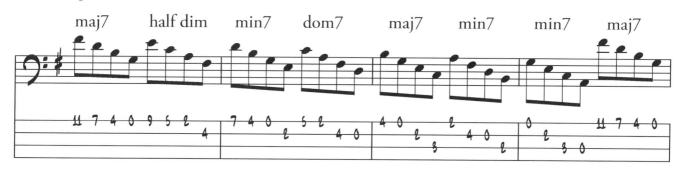

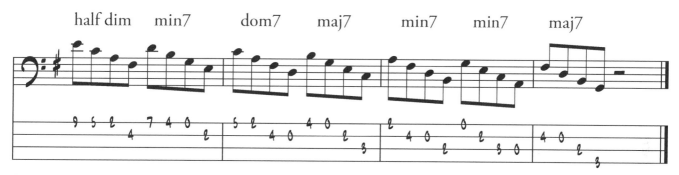

Permutation 2
Ascending & descending

Permutation 3
Down the chord stepwise up the scale

3 Note Groupings

G major scale in triplet groupings
Ascending

Descending

Diatonic 7th Chords in Triplets

D 7 arpeggio

E min7 arpeggio

F# min7 b5 arpeggio

G major arpeggio

Scale studies in the key of Ab Major

Scales, Modes and Arpeggios over 2 octaves

Ab Major scale

Ab maj 7 arpeggio

Bb Dorian scale

Bb min 7 arpeggio

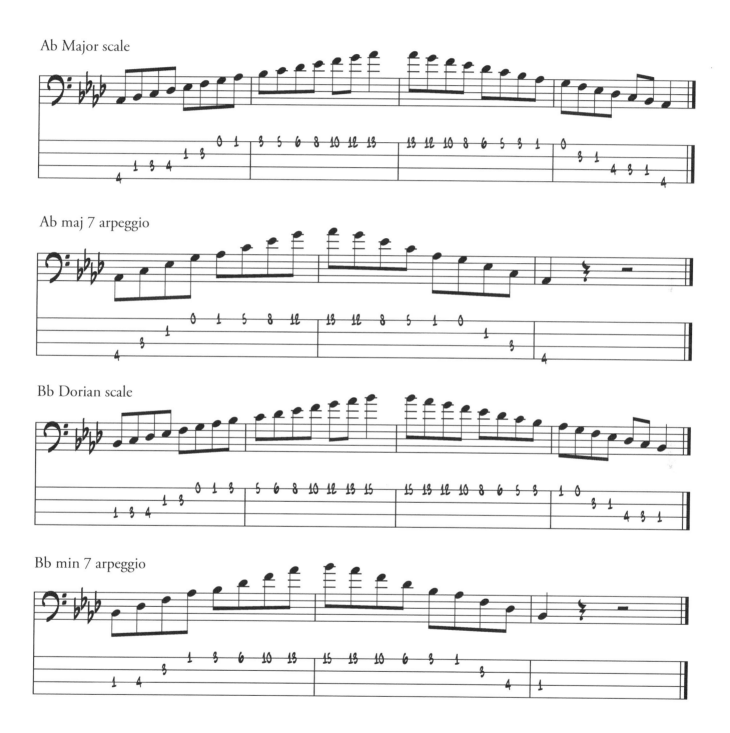

C Phrygian scale

C min 7 arpeggio

Db Lydian scale

Db maj 7 arpeggio

Eb Mixolydian scale

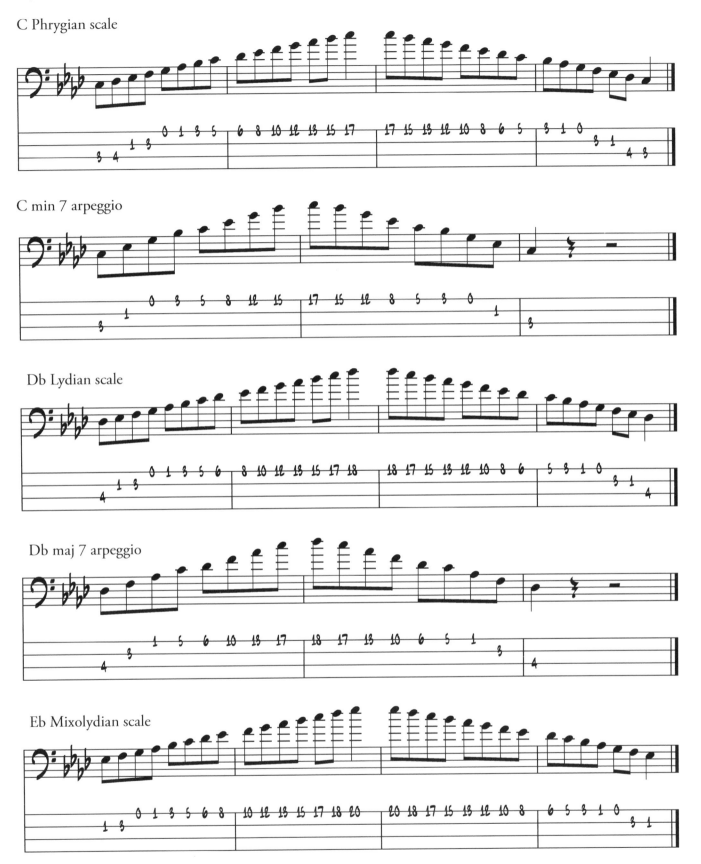

Eb 7 arpeggio

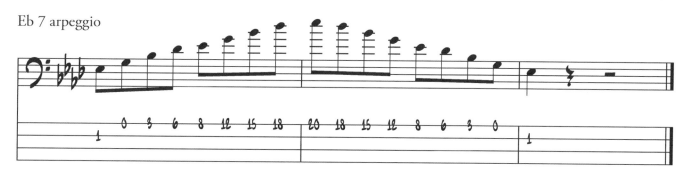

F Aeolian scale

F min7 arpeggio

G Locrian scale

G min7 b5 arpeggio

4 Note Scale Groupings

The following exercise outlines the use of 4 note groupings moving stepwise diatonically through the scale of Ab major.

For example, the 4 note grouping starts on the root note or 1st degree of the scale and progresses stepwise. The exercise then descends from the 2nd octave Ab back to the root.

Ascending

Descending

Permutation 2   Up & Down

As in the previous exercise the following exercise outlines the use of 4 note groupings moving stepwise diatonically through the scale of Ab major.

Notice in exercise #2 the 4 note grouping starts on the root note or 1st degree of the scale and progresses stepwise. In this example we descend when we hit the 5th note in the sequence eg. descending from the 2nd 4 note grouping.

Ascending

Descending

Broken Thirds

Ascending

Descending

4 Note Groupings Diatonic Triads

Ascending 1351

Descending 1351

Ascending 1531

Descending 1531

4 Note Groupings Diatonic 7th Chords

Ascending

Descending

Permutation 2
Ascending & descending

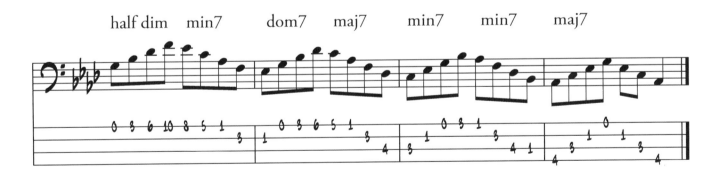

Permutation 3
Down the chord stepwise up the scale

3 Note Groupings

Ab major scale in triplet groupings
Ascending

Descending

Diatonic 7th Chords in Triplets

Ab maj arpeggio

Bb min7 arpeggio

C min7 arpeggio

Db maj 7 arpeggio

Eb 7 arpeggio

F min7 arpeggio

G min7 b5 arpeggio

Ab maj arpeggio

Scale studies in the key of A Major

Scales, Modes and Arpeggios over 2 octaves

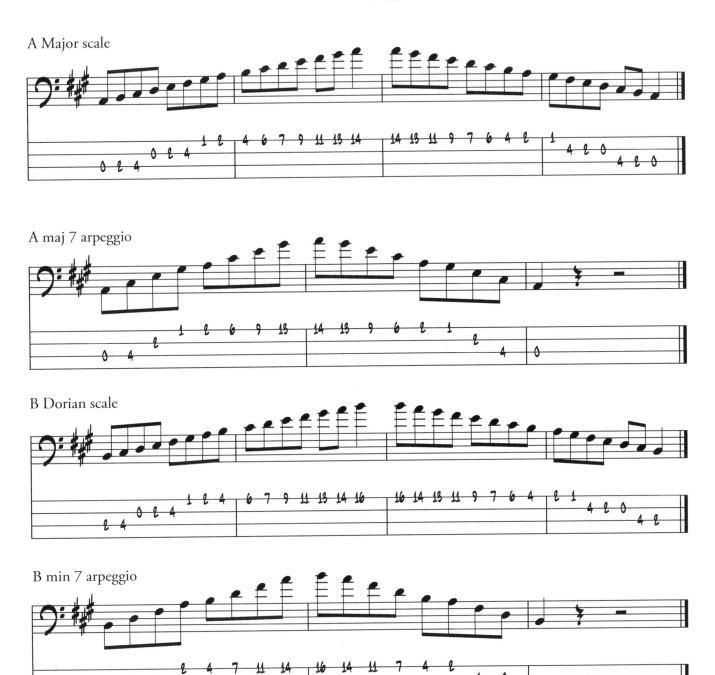

A Major scale

A maj 7 arpeggio

B Dorian scale

B min 7 arpeggio

C# Phrygian scale

C# min 7 arpeggio

D Lydian scale

D maj 7 arpeggio

E Mixolydian scale

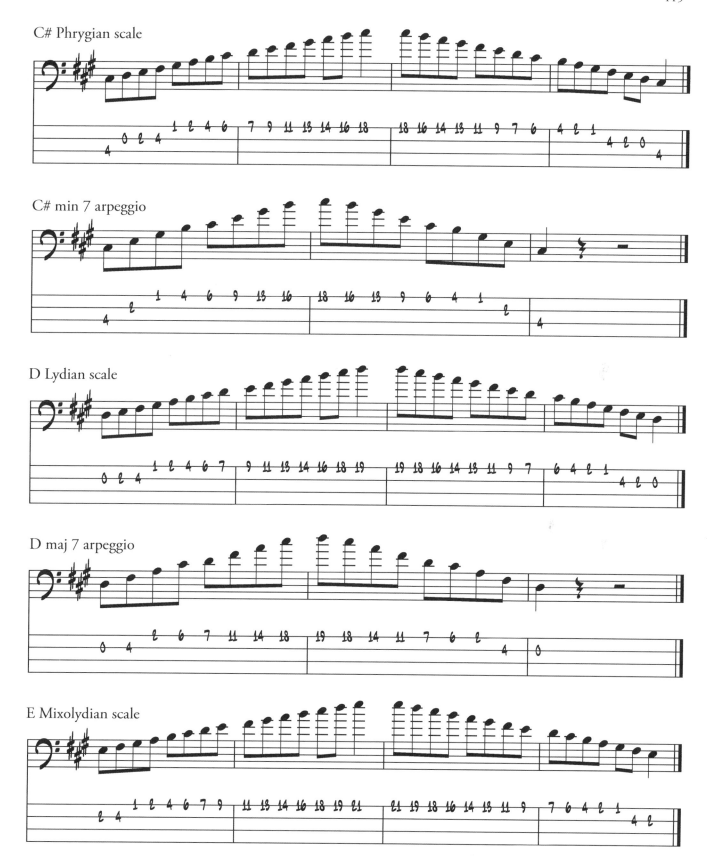

E 7 arpeggio

F# Aeolian scale

F# min7 arpeggio

G# Locrian scale

G# min7 b5 arpeggio

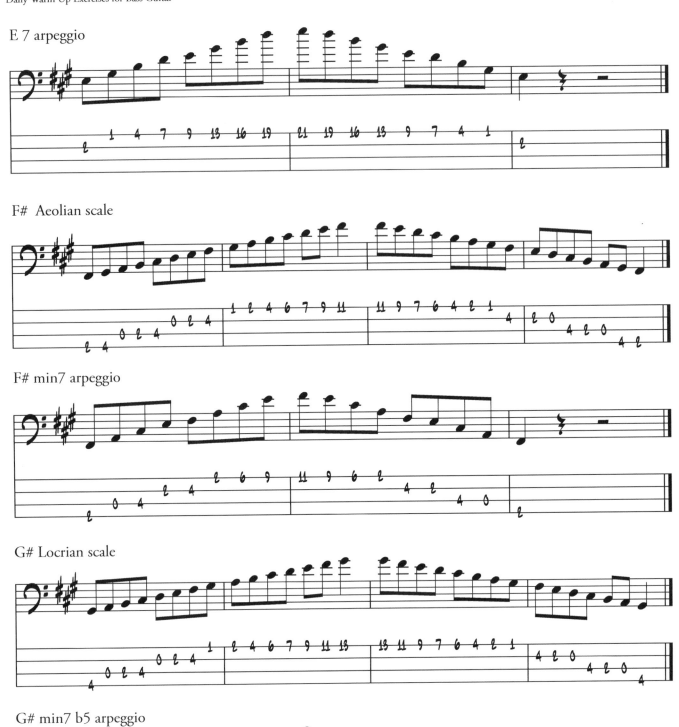

4 Note Scale Groupings

The following exercise outlines the use of 4 note groupings moving stepwise diatonically through the scale of A major.

For example, the 4 note grouping starts on the root note or 1st degree of the scale and progresses stepwise. The exercise then descends from the 2nd octave A back to the root.

Ascending

Descending

Permutation 2

Up & Down

As in the previous exercise the following exercise outlines the use of 4 note groupings moving stepwise diatonically through the scale of A major.

Notice in exercise #2 the 4 note grouping starts on the root note or 1st degree of the scale and progresses stepwise. In this example we descend when we hit the 5th note in the sequence eg. descending from the 2nd 4 note grouping.

Ascending

Descending

Broken Thirds

Ascending

Descending

4 Note Groupings Diatonic Triads

Ascending 1351

Descending 1351

Ascending 1531

Descending 1531

4 Note Groupings Diatonic 7th Chords

Ascending

Descending

Permutation 2
Ascending & descending

Permutation 3
Down the chord stepwise up the scale

3 Note Groupings

A major scale in triplet groupings
Ascending

Descending

Diatonic 7th Chords in Triplets

A maj arpeggio

B min7 arpeggio

C# min7 arpeggio

D maj 7 arpeggio

E 7 arpeggio

F# min7 arpeggio

G# min7 b5 arpeggio

A maj arpeggio

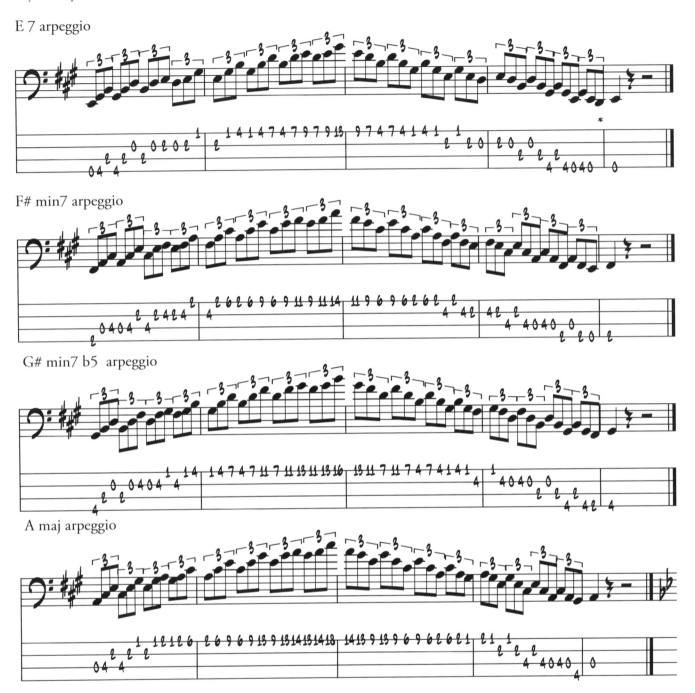

* The D in this exercise is out of the range of the 4 string bass. This passage can
be played 8va eg. 1 octave higher than written

Scale studies in the key of Bb Major

Scales, Modes and Arpeggios over 2 octaves

Bb Major scale

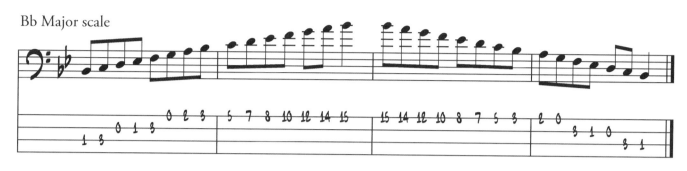

Bb maj 7 arpeggio

C Dorian scale

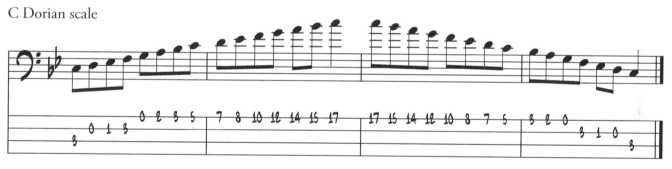

C min 7 arpeggio

D Phrygian scale

D min 7 arpeggio

Eb Lydian scale

Eb maj 7 arpeggio

F Mixolydian scale

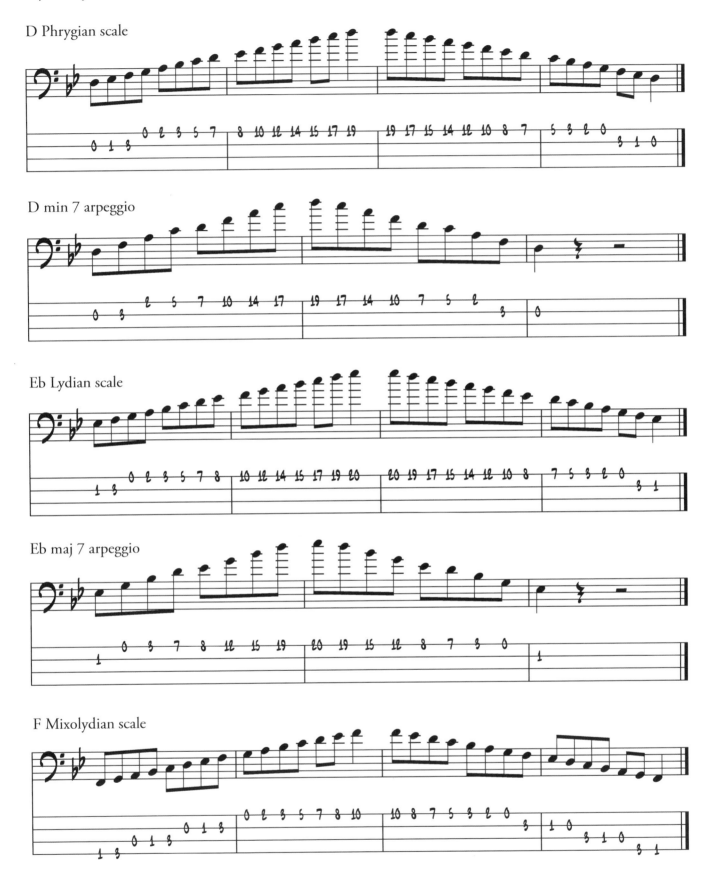

F 7 arpeggio

G Aeolian scale

G min7 arpeggio

A Locrian scale

A min7 b5 arpeggio

4 Note Scale Groupings

The following exercise outlines the use of 4 note groupings moving stepwise diatonically through the scale of Bb major.

For example, the 4 note grouping starts on the root note or 1st degree of the scale and progresses stepwise. The exercise then descends from the 2nd octave Bb back to the root.

Ascending

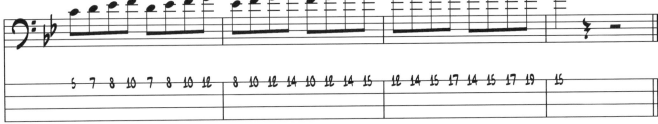

Descending

Permutation 2   Up & Down

As in the previous exercise the following exercise outlines the use of 4 note groupings moving stepwise diatonically through the scale of Bb major.

Notice in exercise #2 the 4 note grouping starts on the root note or 1st degree of the scale and progresses stepwise. In this example we descend when we hit the 5th note in the sequence eg. descending from the 2nd 4 note grouping.

Ascending

Descending

Broken Thirds

Ascending

Descending

4 Note Groupings Diatonic Triads

Ascending 1351

Descending 1351

Ascending 1531

Descending 1531

4 Note Groupings Diatonic 7th Chords

Ascending

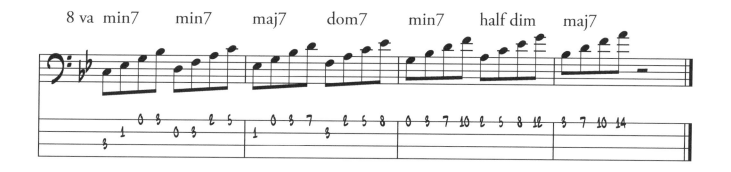

Descending

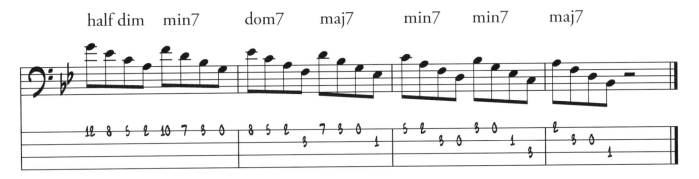

Permutation 2
Ascending & descending

Permutation 3
Down the chord stepwise up the scale

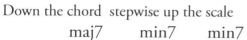

3 Note Groupings

Bb major scale in triplet groupings
Ascending

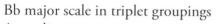

Descending

Diatonic 7th Chords in Triplets

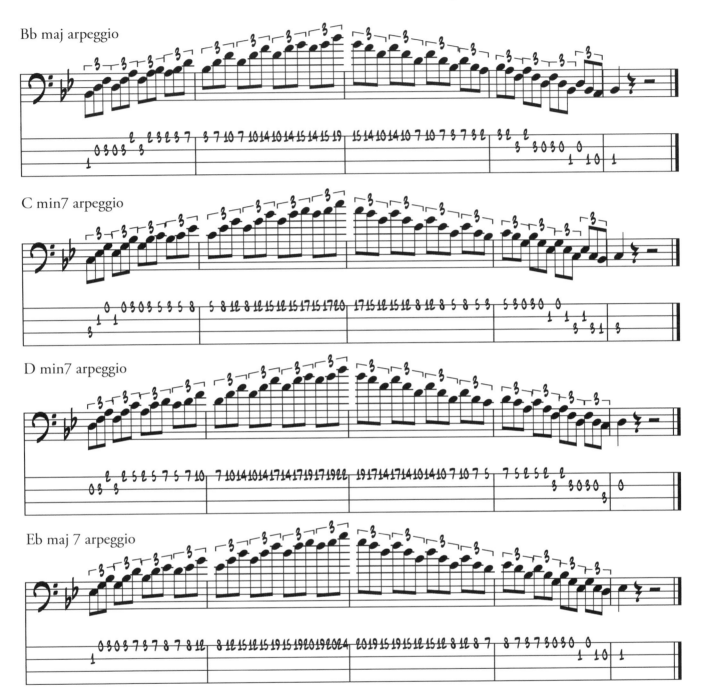

F 7 arpeggio

G min7 arpeggio

A min7 b5 arpeggio

Bb major arpeggio

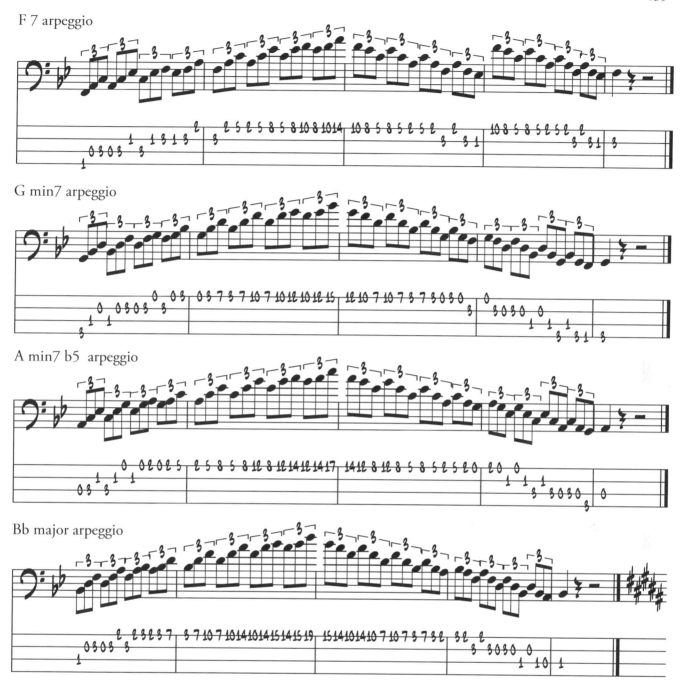

Scale studies in the key of B Major

Scales, Modes and Arpeggios over 2 octaves

B Major scale

B maj 7 arpeggio

C# Dorian scale

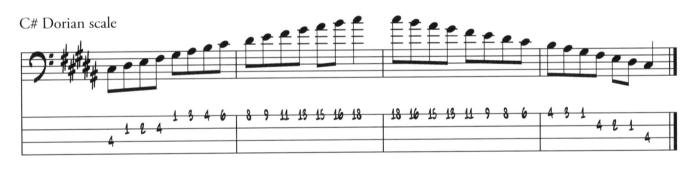

C# min 7 arpeggio

D# Phrygian scale

D# min 7 arpeggio

E Lydian scale

E maj 7 arpeggio

F# Mixolydian scale

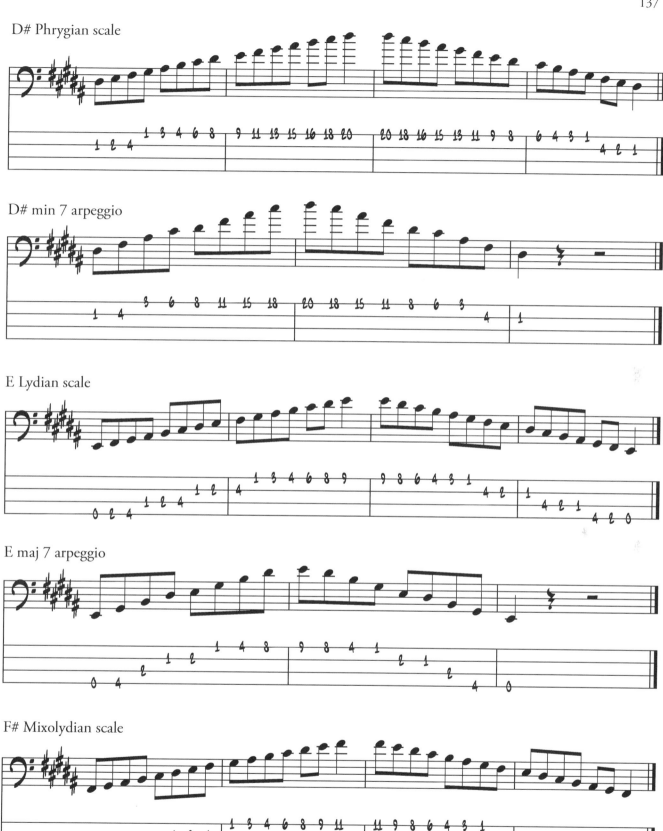

F# 7 arpeggio

G# Aeolian scale

G# min7 arpeggio

A# Locrian scale

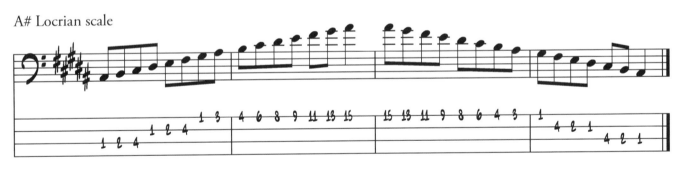

A# min7 b5 arpeggio

4 Note Scale Groupings

The following exercise outlines the use of 4 note groupings moving stepwise diatonically through the scale of B major.

For example, the 4 note grouping starts on the root note or 1st degree of the scale and progresses stepwise. The exercise then descends from the 2nd octave B back to the root.

Ascending

Descending

Permutation 2   Up & Down

As in the previous exercise the following exercise outlines the use of 4 note groupings moving stepwise
diatonically through the scale of B major.
Notice in exercise #2 the 4 note grouping starts on the root note or 1st degree of the scale and progresses
stepwise. In this example we descend when we hit the 5th note in the sequence eg. descending from the
2nd 4 note grouping.

Ascending

Descending

Broken Thirds

Ascending

Descending

4 Note Groupings Diatonic Triads

Ascending 1351

Descending 1351

Ascending 1531

Descending 1531

4 Note Groupings Diatonic 7th Chords

Ascending

Descending

Permutation 2
Ascending & descending

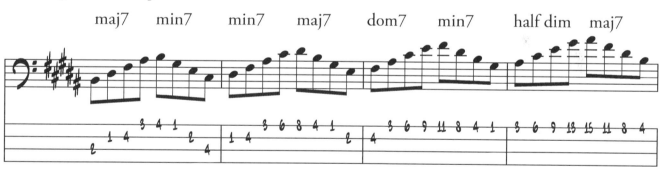

Permutation 3
Down the chord stepwise up the scale

3 Note Groupings

B major scale in triplet groupings
Ascending

Descending

Diatonic 7th Chords in Triplets

Daily Warm Up Exercises for Bass Guitar

F# 7 arpeggio

G# min7 arpeggio

A# min7 b5 arpeggio

B maj arpeggio

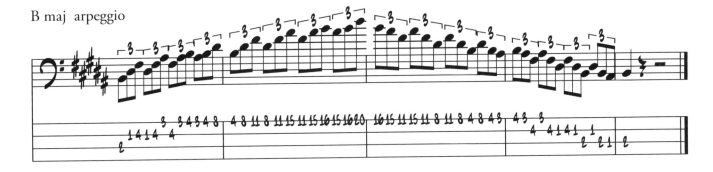

IN CONCLUSION ......

It has been a vast amount of work and dedicated practice that brings the bassist to the last page of this book having covered all the examples within.

It has been the aim of the " Daily Warm Up Exercises " book series to give the aspiring bassist a solid grounding in how to practice in 12 keys and develop a dedicated daily practice routine.

Having covered the material in this book you are now well on your way to finding your own voice as a bassist and as a musician.

For those of you reading the book that are not familiar with reading bass clef, all examples inside the book have been supplied with bass tab and bass clef, use this as a tool to learn to read the bass clef.

There are many opportunities for the reading musician.

Practice the exercises until they become familiar striving for good tone, time and intonation but most importantly - Listen to as much music as you can, Listen to the masters.

The objective has been to make the material for the student as easy to absorb as possible, as a confidance building mechanism.

Your thoughts and comments are important to us and assist us in providing future generations of musicians with quality educational material.

Please send youre thoughts or comments to constructwalkingjazzbasslines@gmail.com

Other books available by Steven Mooney

PRINT EDITIONS

" Constructing Walking Jazz Bass Lines " Book I
Walking Bass Lines : The Blues in 12 Keys

" Constructing Walking Jazz Bass Lines " Book II
Walking Bass Lines : Rhythm Changes in 12 keys

" Constructing Walking Jazz Bass Lines " Book III
Walking Bass Lines : Standard Lines

" Constructing Walking Jazz Bass Lines " Book IV
Building a 12 Key Facility for the Jazz Bassist Book I

" Constructing Walking Jazz Bass Lines " Book V
Building a 12 Key Facility for the Jazz Bassist Book II

Bass Tablature Series

" Constructing Walking Jazz Bass Lines " Book I
Walking Bass Lines : The Blues in 12 Keys -Bass TAB Edition

" Constructing Walking Jazz Bass Lines " Book II
Walking Bass Lines : Rhythm Changes in 12 Keys - Bass TAB Edition

" Constructing Walking Jazz Bass Lines " Book III
Walking Bass Lines : Standard Lines - Bass TAB Edition

" Constructing Walking Jazz Bass Lines " Book IV
Building a 12 Key Facility for the Jazz Bassist Book I - Bass Tab Edition

Coming Soon

Daily Warm Up Exercises for Bass Guitar Pt II - Bass Tab Edition

E-BOOK EDITIONS

All books in the Constructing Walking Jazz Bass Lines series are also available as an eBook for the following reader formats Kindle, iTunes iBookstore, Nook, and Adobe Digital PDF. Follow us on the web for news and new release updates.

http://waterfallpublishinghouse.com

http://constructingwalkingjazzbasslines.com

http://basstab.net

Made in the USA
Lexington, KY
24 October 2013